MW00987055

Hear Us Speak

Suzan Kanoo

Hear Us Speak

LETTERS FROM ARAB WOMEN

ForbesBooks

Published by ForbesBooks, Charleston, South Carolina.
Member of Advantage Media Group.

ForbesBooks is a registered trademark, and the ForbesBooks colophon is a trademark of Forbes Media, LLC.

Printed in the United States of America.

10 9 8 7 6 5 4 3 2 1

ISBN: 978-1-950863-19-8
LCCN: 2020923116

Book design by Megan Elger.

This custom publication is intended to provide accurate information and the opinions of the author in regard to the subject matter covered. It is sold with the understanding that the publisher, Advantage|ForbesBooks, is not engaged in rendering legal, financial, or professional services of any kind. If legal advice or other expert assistance is required, the reader is advised to seek the services of a competent professional.

 Advantage Media Group is proud to be a part of the Tree Neutral® program. Tree Neutral offsets the number of trees consumed in the production and printing of this book by taking proactive steps such as planting trees in direct proportion to the number of trees used to print books. To learn more about Tree Neutral, please visit **www.treeneutral.com**.

Since 1917, Forbes has remained steadfast in its mission to serve as the defining voice of entrepreneurial capitalism. ForbesBooks, launched in 2016 through a partnership with Advantage Media Group, furthers that aim by helping business and thought leaders bring their stories, passion, and knowledge to the forefront in custom books. Opinions expressed by ForbesBooks authors are their own. To be considered for publication, please visit **www.forbesbooks.com**.

To my father, Salman Khalil Kanoo.
God rest his soul. Thank you for believing in me.

And to all of the beautiful, strong women
I was blessed to have met on this journey.

Hear us speak.

Contents

INTRODUCTION: THIS IS UNIVERSAL 1

THE KUWAITI PAINTER. 7

THE BAHRAINI JOURNALIST. 17

THE LONDON HOUSEWIFE 27

THE KUWAITI CEO. 35

THE GCC MOTHER. 43

THE GULF BUSINESSWOMAN. 51

THE KUWAITI INFLUENCER 59

THE GCC SHADOWS. 69

THE ARABIC DAD 77

THE GCC FREE SPIRIT 83

THE SYRIAN REFUGEE 91

THE SAUDI MEDIA ICON 97

THE GCC FIGHTER. 105

LARA, MY DAUGHTER 115

GENERATION Z 119

EPILOGUE: A BRIGHTER TOMORROW. 129

Introduction: This Is Universal

I STARTED THE PROCESS of writing this book to make a difference.

We are all put on this earth for reasons only God knows. Some of us lead happy lives, while others fight battle after battle. In my own life, I've climbed many mountains. Some I have summited. Others I have not.

I love being an Arab woman, and I love the land I was born in. For seven generations, my family has lived in the Kingdom of Bahrain, a small archipelago in the Arabian Gulf. Our culture and history are unique, and for many of our Western neighbors, they remain a mystery.

I'm not here to uncover the mysteries of the Arab world. My country, my culture, my people: we are diverse and dynamic, irreducible to a monolith. My goal is to introduce certain subjects that should be discussed, elevating voices that have often been relegated to the shadows. I believe it is crucial these voices be heard.

My country, my culture, my people: we are diverse and dynamic, irreducible to a monolith.

As I began interviewing Arab women for this book, I was deeply moved by their stories. Many have survived horrific ordeals of physical and emotional abuse. Often, when they appealed to the court system, they were either ignored or told to go back to their abuser. I met women who have been incarcerated for expressing their opinions on social media; women whose husbands kidnapped their children and fled the country; women who worked harder but inherited less than their brothers, simply because they were women.

What struck me most about these stories was not the shock and horror of what the women had endured; it was the fact that they had emerged without hatred or bitterness. These women are strong and capable, thriving in their professional and personal lives. These women have not been crushed by circumstances. They have faced insurmountable odds and survived.

Arab culture is laden with so much inherent beauty. We respect our elders. We raise our children to make the world a better place. But the pace of modernization has outrun the pace of our legislation. It is time to examine certain laws and entrenched belief systems about the rights of women—as mothers, as wives, as citizens—to evolve our way of thinking.

We have built the highest towers in the world, the largest international airports, and the most advanced highways. We have no end of exquisite restaurants and luxurious shopping malls. Yet many of our laws remain unchanged after hundreds of years. For some this is unique and beautiful. For others it causes confusion at best and division, injustice, and suffering at worst.

When I studied abroad in the United States, I was encouraged to think independently. I was invited to form my own opinions, to let go of certain traditions and old ways of thinking. In the West, we are taught our minds and bodies are our own.

Then we return home. Our independence is diminished, and once again we succumb to society's norms and expectations of the rights we have as women. Our individual opinions and thoughts become secondary, because once again we belong to our family or clan.

I am not implying this is sad or negative. A rich history is a treasure, and a sense of belonging is essential for a long, happy life. But we are all global citizens, and I believe it is time to take an honest look at what is working in Arab culture and what isn't. How do we better protect women, especially those who are vulnerable? Do we need new legislation and tougher laws? Are there ways for women to support other women and also rally men to the cause, since they so often occupy positions of power and influence?

It is not my intent to answer these questions for you. Every reader has a right to formulate their own opinions after reading the enclosed letters from Arab women. There is no right or wrong answer; only by discussing these issues openly can we find solutions. My hope is that you will see we are more alike than we are different, and that our humanity is the cord binding us together.

When I first began curating this collection of letters, it was important to me to give voice to *all* Arabic women, not just the most famous ones. I want to talk about the plight we go through and see other women go through. At the end of each chapter, you'll find a brief section entitled "P.S." where I talk more about our culture and our legal system, including some of my own thoughts and opinions. I'm not here to cast judgment or to say "the roles have to change." But I am here to get people to discuss it.

As the letters in this book took shape from the hours of interviews I had with these women, I realized my role was to step back so they could speak. As you'll see, they express their own truths beautifully, sharing their experiences with honesty and bravery. Their stories are powerful. They speak for themselves.

Hear Us Speak is not for everyone. Some of the letters are controversial. Others are painful to read. Often they feel as if something is still being hidden, left out. Many women only felt safe telling me *parts* of their stories, a mere fraction of what happened to them in real life. They have learned to be reserved and silent, to guard their own truths, often because of precisely the same cultural expectations we're questioning in this book. Some of the women we'll hear from have been able to beat the system and fight back; many are still trapped in the shadows, clinging to the briefer moments of light in their lives.

Still, it must be said that significant efforts have already been put forth to empower women in the GCC countries. GCC stands for Gulf Cooperation Council, which is an alliance of six Middle Eastern countries: Saudi Arabia, Kuwait, the United Arab Emirates, Qatar, the Kingdom of Bahrain, and Oman. Since the inception of the GCC, we've seen a lot of progress to empower women, especially in the Kingdom of Bahrain, the Kingdom of Saudi Arabia, and the United Arab Emirates. We've made a good start, but we need to continue to empower women through legislation.

We'll spend a lot of time with women from the GCC. I have done my best to protect the identities of the writers by keeping the letters anonymous. But name or no name, the voice of every single one of these women deserves to be heard. If this book helps even one individual, empowers even one woman, then I have succeeded.

To be a woman is a gift. We give birth to future generations. We give love unconditionally. And we face unique daily challenges and adversity with grace, strength, and courage. This is universal.

Hear us speak.

The Kuwaiti Painter

WHAT I NOTICED FIRST *were the vibrant colors. When we stepped off the elevator and into the room at the end of the corridor, my eyes were treated to a feast of tints and tones: bright scarlet, emerald green, cerulean blue, canary yellow. Swatches of fabric hung from the walls, and on the shelves were dozens of small glass boxes filled with ribbons, buttons, zippers, and clasps. Two lifelike mannequins stood quietly in the costume shop—headless, but perfectly content to be pierced by safety pins, draped in brilliant fabric with glimmering sequins and rich brocade. The woman I'd come to see had made a name for herself as a painter and fashion designer in Kuwait, and as I stood in her studio, I understood why. She had overcome many hardships to achieve what she'd achieved. But I didn't yet know the unthinkable horrors she had endured.*

The Kuwaiti Painter stepped forward and greeted me warmly. She was dressed simply, in linen pants and a blouse dyed a pale shade of olive, her dark hair gathered at the back of her neck. We kissed each other on each cheek: the standard greeting in the Arab world. She had a warmth and steadiness to her movements, and her voice was low and gentle as she ushered me to a plush leather chair.

The room smelled faintly of cigarettes and sweet perfume. We made small talk for a few minutes, then got down to business.

"I wish you'd been here last May," she said. "I had an exhibition about women who have not been recognized by history. They were inventors, chemists, physicists, doctors, and lawyers. Some of them didn't get a Nobel Prize solely because they were Arab women. They had the most incredible stories, ones I'd never heard."

"What about your story?" I asked. "Will you tell it to me?"

She nodded. "I came from an abused background," she began. "It all started with my first husband ..."

The thing is, I'd grown up in a very protective family. Love was the protection; I was protected, but I was also spoiled. No one in my family ever screamed or fought or beat me. Whenever a man came to propose marriage, they would send him away. My family was afraid men would take advantage of my situation and abuse me financially. For them, everything was about the money.

At eighteen I was studying law in Kuwait. I was a quiet, peaceful person, but I'd always been a rebellious dreamer in my thoughts. I wanted to travel, study abroad, work, and get married—preferably in that order.

Then one day a well-respected Kuwaiti woman approached my mother. "You have two daughters," she said. "I have two sons."

I met one of her sons. He had a master's degree from the United States. I thought, "This is my ticket out." I agreed, and we got married after nine months.

The first time he hurt me was three days after our wedding.

It went on for six years.

My husband did things I never could have imagined. He abused me physically, verbally, and emotionally. He took my books away so I couldn't read. He locked me in our house and wouldn't let anyone come to see me, not even my own family. To call it a "house" was generous: it was a hovel with no flooring and no air conditioning. There were times I felt like I would suffocate.

Growing up, I'd always been one of the lucky ones. I came from a good family; we had money and nice things. The other girls often looked at me with envy. They thought, "We can't reach her." And suddenly I was locked in a house with dirt floors, no books, and no visitors.

I was also pregnant.

After my daughter was born, I thought things would get better. They only got worse. My husband was the kind of guy who always kept the house on fire for one reason or another. We all walked on eggshells around him, trying not to make him angry. But my kids suffered. My daughter was always sick. It seemed like every week we were at the hospital.

There were times my husband would throw me into a dark bathroom and lock the door. He would sit beside the door and whisper through the crack, "Kill yourself." For three or four hours he would sit there, saying those words. "Kill yourself. If I were you, I'd kill myself." I felt like I was losing my mind.

My family was in denial. My mother wouldn't talk to me about it, even though she knew something was going on. Every time I escaped my husband's house and went back to my family, telling them I wanted a divorce, they brought me back to him.

The last time he beat me was before the invasion in 1989. My husband was a military guy; the cap he wore had a metal piece on one side. At five o'clock in the morning, he started screaming at the housekeeper. I came downstairs to find this poor woman holding my infant daughter. When I asked my husband what was happening, he struck me in the face with the cap.

The blood wasn't dripping; it was gushing. My daughter started screaming. My face was full of blood, and I couldn't feel anything. But I saw the look on my housekeeper's face.

She was terrified.

Days later, I went to the hospital with a cut on my forehead. It was scabbed over and healing slowly.

"What happened?" the doctor asked.

"I fell down," I told him.

He shook his head. "This is not a falling cut. This was something sharp."

But I was too ashamed to tell him the truth. That's the thing about abusers: they have the power to manipulate you, forcing you to see everything through a thick veil of shame.

Later, I remember walking through the hospital and seeing two police detectives waiting outside a room. I assumed they were keeping an eye on a patient who had committed a crime. I thought, "If I'd come from a bad background, I would go and tell them my husband beat me."

But I wasn't from a bad background. I came from a good family—one of the best in Kuwait City. My family cared about their image, and no one wanted to believe my husband was abusing me. They preferred to look the other way.

Most Arab women have been taught the same thing since we

were born: you shouldn't talk, you shouldn't make noise, and you shouldn't do anything that goes against what your family wants. As a result, we're always trying to put a plaster on our wounds.

But some wounds must see the light. I wasn't going to let myself be forced into a certain image just to satisfy somebody else. When my husband cut my face open, that was it. On July 27, 1989, I left Kuwait for London and took my two children with me.

Shortly after I left for London, my husband's father died. My husband inherited money and he didn't want me to be part of it. That was my ticket out.

I finally had my freedom.

> **Most Arab women have been taught the same thing since we were born: you shouldn't talk, you shouldn't make noise, and you shouldn't do anything that goes against what your family wants.**

In 1992 I came back to Kuwait to live in my grandfather's house with my children. I became another person—bold and aggressive. I'd always been a rebellious dreamer on the inside; now I was rebellious on the outside too. My family had this idea that any woman who left the house after nine o'clock at night was nuts. Proper women had a curfew.

I had no intention of being a proper woman. I partied every night. I'd drive around for hours, finally coming home at midnight. I kept my decency, because I like to be decent, and because after everything I went through, I didn't want to be touched. But I still had to build myself again.

The road back to normal wasn't easy, and it wasn't smooth. After being with a cruel, abusive, toxic man for six years, I didn't even know what "normal" was. I had issues with anger, and I had to work through those issues so I could be a good mother to my children. It's difficult to break the cycle of abuse; most women who go through abuse become abusers. That was certainly true for me. I was manipulating my kids, especially my son, trying to break him because I was broken. Fortunately I was able to get the help I needed. I chose to live my life a different way.

I started working. I was the first grandchild to work in our family, and the first woman too. My aunt took care of my children, and my uncle got me a job at an advertising agency where I learned about client service, marketing, and creative work. I'd always been a person who wanted to learn, and I never backed down from a challenge. My motto became: everything is possible. I still believe that today.

From advertising, I moved into photography department, then into the gallery because my uncle was an artist as well. I had always loved art. One day I asked myself, "Why don't I start painting?" Since then I've never stopped.

I think everything I went through led me to become a painter. There wasn't anywhere else for me to go. I was always trying different things—and suddenly I stepped into the thing I love. When I started painting, it changed me.

Then I became an activist. All those years, I had been giving, giving, giving to other people while waiting for my own expectations to be met. Why not give with *no* expectations? Why not do something for me that made *me* happy?

As I began browsing the web, I was flooded with hope. I found Peace, an organization in the UK. For four years, I worked with them to celebrate peace in Kuwait, creating a beautiful free event for children with art, music, and performance. The donations went to any organization we chose. Today, when other groups and organizations host events, they often ask me if I want to donate a painting, and I'm always happy to be asked. I believe if you give freely and quickly, it will come back without you even asking for it. And of course, when I was asked to be a part of Abolish 153,[1] I immediately said yes. I didn't have to think twice.

Today I help fund the Abolish 153 campaign through an annual art exhibition. I choose the art, curate the show, and do all the fundraising. There is no women's shelter in Kuwait, so with the money we raise from the yearly exhibition, we help women directly. They come to us through our hotline or by word of mouth, and we work to get them out of dangerous living situations. We move them into houses and apartments, help their kids in school, and pair them with lawyers and psychiatrists who work with them pro bono. With every exhibition, we can help four or five abused women.

In a way, it's all come full circle. Thirty years ago, I was one of those women myself.

My kids are grown now. My daughter works in Vienna with the UN, and my son works for a university. I keep myself busy. Even if sometimes I don't see people for days, I'm happy and content. I have my friends, my painting, my activism, and twenty-one cats. After everything I've survived, I've built *me* back again. I don't feel angry anymore. That ended a long time ago.

Today I thank my husband for everything he did to me. It made me strong. I was—*am*—a survivor. Even during the darkest, most frightening hours, I always had hope. Hope that something better lay

---

1   The Abolish 153 campaign refers to dismantling article 153 in Kuwait's penal code, which allows a man to kill a woman if he catches her in a sexual act with someone else.

ahead. Hope that I would one day be free.

For me the word *impossible* doesn't work. I used to say there are only two things that are not possible.

One: to stop death.

Two: to stop *life*.

Sincerely,
The Kuwaiti Painter

P.S.

The thing that struck me most about the Kuwaiti Painter was how she was so full of love. For someone to have gone through everything she went through and be so lovely and forgiving? It was truly inspiring. She wasn't hard. She wasn't jaded. She was not beaten down and angry. As she said to me at the end of our conversation, "I don't feel angry anymore."

Today the Kuwaiti Painter has found her path in life helping others, hosting exhibitions and events that feature the work of other women. While some survivors of abuse might turn inward, she has poured her love outward, using it to make the world a better and warmer place.

The Bahraini
Journalist

SHE ENTERED MY OFFICE SMILING. *Her flowery sundress flowed around her like a soft breeze, her high heels clicking on the hardwood floor. Her trendy triangular sunglasses were opaque—they reflected the light in my office, the mirrored lenses covering deep brown eyes. But I knew those eyes well. They were full of laughter and perseverance. We said hello the Arabic way, a kiss on each check, and I asked her to sit down. The Bahraini Journalist's energy was positive and forthright. She sat and slowly took off her dark sunglasses. Her makeup was thick and perfectly applied.*

"Last time I passed by your office," she said, "you told us you were writing a book about women in the Arab world."

"Yes," I replied.

She lifted her chin, holding her head high.

"I want to tell you my story."

Our eyes locked. Hers were full of complicated emotions. She put her hand on my wrist.

"Before you hear my story, I want you to know two things. The first is that I have proof of everything that happened to me. No one believed me when I told the truth—they thought I was a liar. But I have all the documents."

I leaned forward, intrigued. "And the second thing?"

The Journalist took a breath.

"The second thing is the most important. I am fine, Suzy. I carry no hatred. I have buried all my anger, tears, and disappointments. I am blessed."

She opened her mouth … and told me a story I could never have imagined.

When I was a little girl, my parents divorced. This was unusual; it was a time when most people did not get divorced. But my parents did, and after they separated, I mostly lived with my father and stepmother.

It didn't take me long to realize I was trapped in a Cinderella story. At five o'clock every morning, my stepmother woke my two brothers, my sister, and me … with her feet. "Go wash the bathrooms," she'd say, kicking us awake. "Go clean the windows." I'd come home from school every afternoon and put on my cleaning uniform. "Go wash the garden," she'd say. "Go scrub the floors."

When I tried to do my reading for school, she scoffed. "Books won't give you a future." She pointed at a dusty windowsill. "*That's* what will give you a future. The dust." As if the only way to make something of myself was to scrub and mop and clean.

Even when my stepmother cooked nice food, she'd keep it for herself and my father. My siblings and I had to find other food. It was so depressing that my oldest brother went to live with my grandmother. My older sister left Bahrain for a while. My youngest brother ran away, started doing drugs, and died alone on the street.

I didn't run away. Unlike my siblings, I stayed. I split my time between my mother's house and my father's house, where my stepmother continued to abuse me. I tried to be patient, to survive all these things, and I helped out wherever I could.

Then I met my Prince Charming.

I thought this man was my escape, my way out of an abusive home. My father didn't care if I got married, but my mother and stepmother did not approve. "I feel he's not good for you," my mother said.

"But he loves me," I replied.

When my husband forced their hand by convincing me to give myself to him before marriage, I should have known something was wrong.

"Now you have to say yes," he told my parents. "No one else will want her."

They agreed.

I was married at twenty years old.

After the wedding, my husband and I moved into his family house. After a year, I still wasn't pregnant. He started to get bored. Since he worked in tourism, he began to work longer hours, staying away from home more and more. There were Russian girls who came to the hotel, dancers. He was supposed to take care of me, but he left me with his family while he went out and had his fun.

Then he took his fun too far. He was called to the army but did not go to war. In the United States, they would call this dodging the draft. The Bahraini police caught him. He was in jail for several years.

That's when I got pregnant.

When I gave birth to our first daughter, they discharged my husband from jail so he could be there for the birth. But when I went into labor, he said he was too tired. He was still sleeping when my neighbor took me to the hospital to deliver our child.

Later, when he saw our beautiful baby girl, he was angry.

"You're a donkey," he shouted. "You brought me a girl, not a boy."

But I still had hope. *Maybe she will have a good life*, I told myself.

I started to gain weight. I fed my daughter in bed, and sometimes, when I felt too lifeless to do anything, I slept.

"How can you feed the baby when you are sleeping on her?" he shouted.

"She's beside me when I sleep. I know how to take care of my baby."

He started beating me after that.

He beat me when I fed her and when I didn't. When she woke up in the night, crying for milk, he beat me and shouted for her to stop.

"Babies cry," I said.

"Get out," he snarled. "I don't want to hear it."

But we only had one room in the house. There was nowhere for me to go.

He wasn't taking care of us. I didn't have a phone or a car. He refused to let me see my family, so my own mother hadn't met her granddaughter. Sometimes I thought about what she'd said two years earlier. "I don't want you to marry this man," she'd told me.

"But he loves me," I'd replied. "Right now I have to choose any open door."

I was pregnant with my second baby when I got the news that my mother was sick. My husband wouldn't let me see her. In the midst of my grief, I kept trying to take care of my babies. One morning I left the house to buy Pampers and formula, and when my husband caught me outside, he beat me. I'd never reported it when he beat me at home—I knew no one would believe me. But after he beat me in public, I went to the police and filed a report. This time, other people saw him do it.

So I went to court. After hearing my husband's side, the judge sided with him. My husband took me home and raped me. He changed the lock and put a seal on the windows. I could not contact anybody. My mum was in the hospital with cancer, and I couldn't go see her. My family thought I was a bad wife, a bad mother, and a bad daughter for not asking about my family. But they didn't know the truth. Even when I tried to tell them, they never believed me. They didn't know I was being held prisoner in our house. That my husband kept beating me and bringing home another woman, making me watch while they had sex in our bed. Our daughter saw it too.

I knew I had to escape. My daughter and the baby growing inside me deserved a better future. A better life.

Whenever my husband fell asleep after having sex with the other woman, he kept a little gold key in his clothes. I knew the only way to get the key was to sleep with him. I didn't want to do this—the idea made me sick. But I wanted to survive. I wanted my daughters to survive.

So I slept with him. Once he was asleep, I took the key. I crept to the door, praying that my little girl would not open her mouth and cry.

It was three o'clock in the morning when I slipped out of the house. I didn't have a telephone, and we lived in a part of town with no taxis.

And then a miracle happened. A taxi drove down the street. I waved him down and begged him to take me to my mother's house. I didn't have any money, but I promised I'd be able to pay him once I got there. My mum was still in the hospital, but my sister was at the house and gave me the money for the taxi. I told her I wanted to see our mum.

"No," she said. "Mum is dying. You think you can just breeze back in after all these months and see her?"

A week later, my mother died.

I never got to say goodbye.

It took six years to divorce my husband. Every time the police tried to deliver the papers, they couldn't find him. He kept moving and changing his address. And still the courts told me, "You have to wait. We need his approval to grant the divorce. He's allowed to cancel it."

The man who was beating me … who had imprisoned me in our home … who made me watch while he had sex with another woman … who barred me from seeing my family as my mother was dying—he was still allowed to cancel the divorce.

He tried to take our second daughter away from me. But at least that time, the courts were on my side. "How can you take a baby from her mother?" they said, and ruled in my favor.

For six years, I waited. Neither of my children had passports, because they couldn't have any formal documents without him. I was so angry. How could he be a father? A husband? How could he do all these horrible things?

Every day was a battle. To get child support. To feed and clothe my daughters. And every day, I went to war. Every day I said, "I have to find a way." My mind, my heart: I was always thinking of my daughters. For them, I would fight every day, forever.

And finally, six years later, we won the war.

For a long time, I was angry. But I don't think about the anger anymore. I think about how to survive, how to live my life. If I want to be happy, I have to think about the future instead of the past. So I throw myself into my work, or I make plans for my daughters. I think about their studies. I think about how to get them passports, since the law still requires their father to be present to apply.

> **If I want to be happy, I have to think about the future instead of the past.**

My daughters are twenty-two and twenty now. The eldest is married to a good man. The youngest is in college and thriving. There are so many things that make me happy, so many things to think about. If I keep sitting with the anger, I will not reach for the solution.

I am a fighter. I have learned to love myself. I had to be patient and intelligent about how to survive. If all you think about is the pain, then you will stay in the pain. So you have to open your mind. You have to find your own path, to reach beyond the pain and the anger if you want to live.

At twenty I thought there was only one door. I thought I couldn't ask for anything better. But you always have a choice. There are so many doors … and so many keys.

Sincerely,
The Bahraini Journalist

P.S.

I was inspired by the Bahraini Journalist's story of strength and perseverance. "I carry no hatred," she told me. I found that lovely. Maybe it's true what the spiritual people always say: forgive people, because it is the only way to leave hatred behind you.

The Bahraini Journalist came from a basic family. She did not grow up with wealth or connections, and she had no one helping her. She went through all of this on her own. But she was determined to give her daughters a better life. She fought to see the light at the end of the tunnel—and to reach it.

Some people might look at an Arabic woman who is a CEO or in another position of power and think, "She is the kind of strong woman I would like to admire." And those women certainly deserve to be admired. But I think women who have gone through all of these hardships who are not *necessarily in positions of power—and who still look at the future with optimism and a smile—also deserve our admiration and respect. They are the unsung heroes, the voices we so rarely hear. I feel blessed to be part of their journeys too.*

The London
Housewife

I LOVE LONDON. *Every time I go to visit my son at university, I relish my time in the city: the crispness in the air, the fine restaurants and shops, the picturesque red double-decker buses zipping up and down the streets.*

So when I had the opportunity to meet with an Arab woman who'd been living in London for some time, I leapt at it. "You'll definitely want to hear her story," said our mutual friend.

The London Housewife and I sat side by side on a bench in Hyde Park, the surrounding trees awash in rich autumnal colors. She wore a gray wool peacoat. Her face was round, half hidden behind dark-framed glasses. She was clearly well educated and intelligent, and she spoke quietly, often looking down at the fallen leaves beneath us. Whenever a jogger or a group of camera-toting tourists walked past, she lowered her voice, as if she didn't want anyone to hear her story.

We were virtual strangers, she and I. And yet, in a way, we were sisters, Arab women far from home. We came from the same part of the world—and were fully aware of what that meant, both the good and the bad.

"But surely in London, your experience was different than it would have been back home?" I said.

Her smile was sad.

"At first I believed that too."

I met him in my late twenties. He was tall, handsome, and charming.

I had a successful career that gave me a lot of self-esteem. My parents come from a middle-class family; they are educated and well respected in our society. They provided my sister and me with everything we needed: love, emotional support, and a good education. As it is the culture of my country, I was still living with my parents.

He was at the beginning of his professional career, very ambitious and ready to conquer the world. We fell in love and decided to get married. My parents were opposed to the idea, due to the difference in our social status. They did not believe he would be able to offer me the kind of life and lifestyle they'd been able to provide.

But I insisted, and we got married. We lived very close to his parents. I couldn't cope with them—they were superficial and narrow-minded. But who cares when you are married to the love of your life?

I was still working and helping him with the house bills. I didn't think twice about it. We were at an early stage of our lives, and as husband and wife, it didn't really matter who paid for what. I even supported the house fully when he was between jobs, and also paid for his courses so he could become a certified accountant. We had our children in that house. We had a nice life and made good friends. We were happy.

Or at least, I thought we were.

A few years passed. We decided to move to London after he received a tempting job offer. This meant I had to leave my family, friends, and most importantly, my successful career. But I must admit that the idea of living in London was appealing, and it was our mutual decision to make this move.

It was challenging at the beginning, me at home alone, handling the children with no one to help me. But he was there during the weekends, and he made sure we explored the city and had fun. We built a nice community around us. I'm a very outgoing person, just like him; I made sure to maintain strong relationships with our friends and have them over regularly. This required spending a lot of time in the kitchen preparing and cleaning, but the pleasure of having people over outweighed all the physical and mental effort. I didn't work in London—and he never asked me to—because being a mom in London was a full-time job. He was growing at work, and he was very proud of himself. I was proud of him too.

The London busy life means that you don't have a lot of time to take care of yourself. If you're coming from a pace where you regularly have time to do your nails or your hair, those things become less of a priority in this city. I didn't exercise much and started to gain weight. He didn't like the change and commented about it a few times. I didn't think it was a big deal. If you love someone, would it matter if they gain or lose ten kilograms? It shouldn't. Our intimate life was not as active as it used to be, but isn't that the case for all married couples?

My husband's job was very stressful, and he became less happy.

He would complain a lot about it. Over a couple of months, we grew distant.

And then one day he asked if we could talk. I knew he was going to complain about his work. But he had another surprise for me. He told me he was not happy with me, and that he'd been feeling that way for a long period of time. He told me he had never loved me. He said I didn't take care of myself and I didn't take care of him. He said I was not ambitious because I didn't work in London. He said I had no friends. He said I was miserable and I was the reason he was unhappy.

But that was only the beginning.

He told me he was seeing someone else—and that he loved her. She made him happy. She satisfied his needs.

I was shocked. I couldn't believe the words coming out of his mouth. He was so comfortable talking about it, making sure to blame me for the unsuccessful marriage, although he had never mentioned he was unhappy with me.

I was shocked and devastated—and took all the blame. I believed him. I regretted being what I was. I hated myself. I was convinced I was the reason behind this. He made me believe every single word he said. I could not talk to anyone about it for weeks, not even my parents. What would I tell them? The man I insisted to marry and whom they opposed had left me for another woman?

Days passed. I spent them at home crying and taking the blame every night he came home after work. Finally I needed to talk, so I told my family and then a couple of friends.

While I was suffering, he was enjoying his new love. And then I saw a new ring on his finger. I asked him if he married her and he said yes. Another wave of shock, denial, regret, and depression.

But why *not* marry another woman, if your religion allows you to?

A lot was going on my mind. The feeling of regret was slowly fading, as I started to realize what he did was shameful and he couldn't blame me for it. But I was always depressed. I stopped talking to most of my friends. I gained a lot of weight. I started to have health issues. I could not take care of the children as much as I used to. I

But why *not* marry another woman, if your religion allows you to?

didn't feel like going back home, because I was dreading the looks on other people's faces when they saw me.

My husband was Muslim, but he had never practiced much. When we used to entertain people and have friends over, he would drink alcohol. But suddenly he became *very* religious—or at least, pretended to. He never missed a prayer and preached about Islam constantly: the religion that gave him a green card to do what he did to me. He forgot about the essence of Islam. He was a bad person willing to hurt everyone around him, including his own children, for his own satisfaction. He neglected the house and our children. They do not love him anymore. They're actually ashamed of him, and very cautious that their non-Muslim friends do not know their dad is married to two women.

I am still not me. I'm not stable emotionally. I hate him for what he did to us, to me and to our children. But I still live with him because that was the best option for me. He mentions his new wife regularly as if I was his sister. I still do his laundry; I still cook his dinner.

He destroyed me. It took a lot of strength for me to get rid of the self-blame, and I still constantly think of what I could or should have done differently to avoid this situation. I am very lonely. And miserable.

He is very successful in his career, and he denies that I supported him throughout his journey. He spends a lot of money on the new wife and questions every time I use his credit card, although most of it is related to the house and the children. I don't know if he is happy or not. All I know is that he has no sense of guilt at all. On the contrary, he did what his religion allowed him to. And in our culture, no one has the right to blame his decision.

Sincerely,
The London Housewife

P.S.

Not every letter in this book has a happy ending. Many of these women are still working through a lot of pain and anger; they are in the middle of their stories. But I believe voices like the London Housewife's deserve to be heard. This woman came from an affluent family and moved to the West with her husband. She thought she had it all. Now she is understandably disappointed at what life has thrown her way. She was doing her best as a wife and mother. How could this have happened when she was taking such great care of her beautiful children? She feels like she has somehow failed.

I believe she did not *fail. She raised her children well. She took care of her husband. Just because a woman gains a little weight or doesn't look like a supermodel does not give her husband a right to look elsewhere. The double standard is so evident here. When husbands gain weight and don't take care of themselves, most wives do not go off and find other men!*

There is a lot of pressure on today's women to be the perfect mothers, have the perfect figures, and work the perfect jobs. I think this is true in any country, not just Arab ones. Social media certainly isn't helping. The London Housewife did everything to her utmost. She thought she ticked all the boxes, and yet this happened to her anyway. Sometimes it just happens.

The Kuwaiti CEO

WE DROVE IN A JEEP TO THE CEO'S OFFICE. *The streets of Kuwait City were crowded with warehouses and offices mixed together. Sand-colored structures in the Ottoman style stood next to contemporary office buildings boasting tall glass windows and slate-gray floors. It was a juxtaposition of old and new, a blend of ancient tradition and modern progress.*

As the elevator doors opened, we stepped into an office with an artistic, industrial feel. The aesthetic was crisp and clean; beautifully designed posters lined the walls, showcasing projects from the company's impressive portfolio.

And there, standing in the hall, was the woman we had come to see: the Kuwaiti CEO.

"Thank you for coming," she said, greeting us in perfect English. "It's so nice to meet you."

She was pretty and professional, dressed in a lovely tailored suit. She ushered us into the meeting room, where my team and I sat on one side of the long glass table, and she and her assistant sat facing us. Water and tea were served.

I thanked her for meeting with us and being part of this book, explaining how happy I was to interview such a successful professional woman. She was humble and elegant in her demeanor and words.

"It's an absolute pleasure to have you here," said the Kuwaiti CEO. "I am inspired by you and everything you've done. It's always such a pleasure to sit in front of women who have really helped shape the trajectory of where we're hoping to go. It's an honor and privilege to have you all here today."

I told her that my goal in this book was not to highlight my own journey, but that of Arab women, many of whom live in the shadows.

To my surprise, the CEO replied, "I think the shadows can be an empowering place to be."

I find that women have played an incredible role here in Kuwait. Not just in shaping how society works, but really how society builds itself moving forward. In the past, women may have lived in the shadows, but we like to say we've excelled so much that if we had a Marvel character, she'd be named Shadow Woman. We would be the ones who live in the shadows because we find that empowers rather than weakens us.

There are advantages to living and working in the shadows. It gives us a bit more leeway, a bit more space to be creative and work under the radar, rather than always being up front and center, 100 percent on, on, on, on. I think we as women use our femininity—and I say this in front of the men here—to drive forward our wants and needs. We do that quite cleverly in some cases, which I believe is a superpower of women, both in the spotlight and in the shadows.

Our sense of nurturing plays a significant role. Women are mothers, even those of us who don't have our own children. Our tendency to nurture helps drive us forward in everything we do. I had the pleasure of running the ministry of youth here in Kuwait, a newly created government agency. Remarkably, a majority of the population of Kuwait is under the age of thirty-four—even I was only in my mid-thirties when I took the position. Overnight I felt like I became the mother of all these young men and women. It was an incredible honor and privilege to have that sense of responsibility.

I don't think men can nurture, at least not in the same way. Men tend to look at the politics rather than the emotional elements. Being a woman gave me a huge advantage: I was able to really dig deep into the youth population and say, "I understand what you're going through on an intrinsic level. Let's look at what affects you as young men and women."

That's how we started to create the building blocks of society: by nurturing these young men and women. It didn't feel like I was going to work; it felt like home. I believe we women have a kind of sixth sense that, unfortunately, I haven't seen in many men. I embrace my sex, my femininity—and I make sure I work it all to my advantage to benefit society at large.

As I helped shape the youth ministry, we were able to build a workforce from scratch. I'm proud to say women comprised 67 percent of my team. These young women really understood what it took to build an agency from scratch—and they were ready to go onto the battlefield with me, because it was definitely a battlefield when I took office. We're a very vocal society here in Kuwait, very political—and very proud of it. But around the time the ministry came to be, there were demonstrations in the street. Young men and women were demanding change. His Highness felt that, since these people had something to say, we should provide an official platform for them to say it. I was brought in to be that platform.

I didn't come in with an iron fist. I literally sat on the sidewalk and listened to these young men and women. I learned so much from them. Today, forty-seven of the people who were heading the demonstrations in the street work inside the ministry, including four top leaders in the government sector.

There will always be a shadow you can step out of; there are times life requires you to step out of your comfort zone. But sometimes

> **There will always be a shadow you can step out of; there are times life requires you to step out of your comfort zone. But sometimes there's a shadow that you need to step back *into*, to recharge.**

there's a shadow that you need to step back *into*, to recharge. There's a certain comfort in that, something I understand and appreciate more now that I'm outside of public office. The shadow can be a great space to create. For me it has always occupied a very sacred place inside me, a place where I could check in with myself and understand what my priorities were, find my inner strength so I could come back out and serve again.

The shadow was always my superpower. It can be a place for women to find our true north so we don't lose ourselves. Sometimes you have to retreat into the shadow before stepping back into the light.

On June 26, 2015, tragedy struck in Kuwait. A suicide bomber walked into a Shia mosque and detonated a bomb in the middle of Friday prayers. The terrorist attack was all the more devastating during the holy month of Ramadan. The mosque was at peak capacity. Twenty-seven people were killed and 227 were wounded.

Friday is the weekend for us, much like Sunday in the United States: a time to rest and recharge and be with family. When the bombing happened, we weren't at the ministry of youth. My team and I were at home. We found ourselves scrambling, first of all to make sense of it. How had this happened? *Why* had this happened? When tragedy strikes, it's easy to become paralyzed.

But within minutes, I was in my car. I was minister of youth, mind you, not minister of information or communication or defense or interior. But that meant nothing. All I could think was how to help and serve using the strengths I had. Everybody was terrified, because we didn't know if there was another bomb; people who had lived through the invasion in 1990 said they had the same sick, heavy feeling in their stomach. It was a very scary time.

Within thirty minutes, His Excellency went to the mosque himself. There is a formal procedure for when he visits any new place; the area is cordoned off the day before so the guards can do a security check and put other protective measures in place. And yet His Excellency walked right into a recently bombed site, not knowing whether there were additional bombers or booby traps, because he felt like he needed to be there.

I felt like I needed to be there, too, in a different way. The media wasn't stepping up or talking about what had happened. None of the other ministers were stepping up, and I knew in my heart that the people of Kuwait needed to hear somebody from the government say something, to deliver a message not just of comfort, but of unity and strength.

Before I joined government, I worked in film and TV. Faced

with a crisis, I went back to my roots. I drove to an office building right next door to the mosque, where one of my team members had a small studio.

In under an hour, and working with a skeleton crew, we filmed a public service announcement. The setup was simple: it was just me, speaking directly to the camera. I let the audience know that we stood together, united and unafraid. That we would not let this act of terror divide us. I said there was no difference between Shiites and Sunnis in Kuwait, and whoever wanted to create that image would be defeated. My message was crystal clear.

We posted the video on social media an hour and a half after the bombing. It immediately went viral. Soon the video became a national campaign: we brought in fifteen other people after me. It was almost surreal, stepping into my own power, knowing exactly what I had to do. All my years of training and experience came together and I knew *how* to do it. I put together strong messaging and galvanized my team. We were there to support the Kuwaiti people, to give them whatever we could. And that's exactly what we did.

I'm not a Marvel superhero, but I do have a certain set of strengths and skills I can call on to help the people I serve.

The very skills I learned in the shadows.

Sincerely,
The Kuwaiti CEO

P.S.

The Kuwaiti CEO was very sophisticated and politely elegant in the way she spoke, and it was an honor to meet a woman of her stature who has done so much in life.

When I meet other female CEOs, I always like to acknowledge how hard they have worked. I think to myself, I know what you've gone through. I've gone through the same thing. *Even if we don't talk about it directly, deep down I know. Whether or not we admit it, we both understand, just by looking into each other's eyes, that our paths were not easy. It* is *a man's world.*

The Kuwaiti CEO and I have been lucky enough to achieve what we've achieved. But we have worked extremely hard and persevered. I don't think there was a single day that was easy. Even if a last name does sometimes open the door, we have to achieve. In fact, women must often overachieve *to gain the professional respect of those around us. I get to the office every day by seven o'clock in the morning just to make a point. I am essentially saying, "I'm here. I'm not lazy. I'm a professional." Now it has become a trait. Women must often work doubly hard to gain the same respect as men.*

One thing I have learned through the process of compiling these letters is that women are strong. In the last section of this book, you'll hear Generation Z say, "Power to women!" I said "Yes!" I'm so impressed by how strong women are. Sometimes we underrate ourselves, but we are so strong. And not just in our region—the whole world. We women are so much stronger than we think.

The GCC Mother

I MET THE GCC MOTHER IN MY LAWYER'S OFFICE. *She was of medium height, in her mid-thirties, with olive skin and a headscarf covering her hair.*

She looked tired, dark circles under her eyes. As we spoke, she kept looking around her, as if she was frightened someone might overhear, even though we were in a safe space.

But mostly she looked sad. The only time the light came into her brown eyes was when she told me about her two sons.

"They're everything to me," she said, and I could tell how much she loved them. "But because of the law, I can't give them what they deserve. They don't have passports. They have no citizenship. They cannot go to university. They have never travelled; they might not travel. I cannot imagine how they will make a life or have a family."

The GCC Mother was becoming agitated. She stood up and paced the room.

"Would you be comfortable starting at the beginning?" I asked. She nodded, her eyes full of tears.

My cousin was a handsome man. For years I'd heard my mother speak favorably of him. She would dole out little details about the way he looked—"Tall!" "Beautiful brown eyes!"—and the kind of work he did.

I barely remembered him. He was from a more affluent part of the family, and because he lived in another country in the GCC, I hadn't seen him since I was a child.

"You were too young," my mother told me. "But if you're lucky, you will meet again."

When I was sixteen, we *did* meet again, at a family gathering. It was love at first sight. I was shy and naive; he swept me off my feet. Falling in love was the easiest thing I'd ever done.

A few weeks later, he asked me to be his wife.

"Marry me," he said. "You'll make me the happiest man alive."

He was the man of my dreams. And not just mine. There are so many stories of women falling in love with men and their parents disapproving of the marriage. But that wasn't the case for me. My mother and father were so happy. He was the man of their dreams, too.

"You are lucky," my mother told me on my wedding day. "Cherish everything you have."

The first three months of our marriage were beautiful. I had everything I'd ever dreamed of and more. We travelled the world, reveled in breathtaking scenery, and met fascinating people. I loved building a home with him. Every night we'd sit by the pool in our backyard, staring up at the night sky. We talked about starting a family, dreaming about the kind of life we would provide our children.

After the honeymoon phase had passed, things started to go bad. I don't know why. The first abuse was verbal. When I didn't cook a meal the way he wanted me to cook it, he began mocking me, calling me names. It took me completely by surprise. He'd never spoken to me that way before. I tried to dismiss it, thinking perhaps he'd a bad day at work.

But the verbal abuse continued. It was unrelenting. If the house wasn't clean enough, he would berate me for being a horrible wife. If the house was sparkling clean, he would berate me for spending too much time cleaning and not enough with him. I could do nothing right.

He told me I was worth nothing because my family was poor. That hit me like a dagger in the heart. He constantly reminded me that his family was unhappy he didn't live with them, angry that he wasn't even in his home country. They were disgusted that he had married "beneath" him. As the insults kept coming, my self-worth rapidly deteriorated; I felt pressured to do something, anything, to make it better.

So I got pregnant. That was the advice I got from everyone. I desperately hoped this would make him happy. Now I recognize this as a delusion, but I *was* delusional. I didn't know how to make him treat me better. Divorce, of course, was not an option, since it would mean that I would be disgraced somehow, even if it wasn't my fault. I thought surely if I were the mother of his child he would love me again.

Nine months later, I gave birth to a beautiful boy.

That was when the physical abuse started.

I wish I could say I fought him. I wish I could tell you that I told someone what he did to me, instead of hiding the bruises with makeup or under my abaya. Sometimes he hit me with his hands. Other times he used hard objects—plastic, wood, even metal.

I knew what my husband was doing was wrong, but I was frightened of what he would do to my son if I spoke up. Would he take him away from me? Or would he do something worse? Surely he would not hurt our child. But the man I fell in love with had turned into someone I didn't recognize. I no longer knew what he was capable of—and I never wanted to find out.

The abuse only got worse. And yet, despite the horrors and endless emotional and physical abuse I lived through every day, I still wanted him to love me. I wasn't thinking clearly, which I now understand to be completely normal when you are being abused, threatened, and traumatized every day. At the time, I did not know this. I felt shame over how much I yearned to have the man I married look at me the way he had on those starlit nights when we sat by the pool, dreaming about the family we would someday create together.

I felt desperate to create that perfect family. Maybe it wasn't too late. Surely it would bring him back to himself, resurrecting the loving husband and father I'd always believed he would be. So I got pregnant again.

And everything fell apart.

Before my second son was born, my husband told me he wanted to divorce me. One day he simply looked at me and said, "You are divorced." In my country, if a husband wants to divorce his wife, he needs only to say those words. Later he can go to court and tell them he spoke those words, and they will give him a letter to send to his wife, making the divorce official.[2]

---

2   In Sharia law, a man can divorce his wife by stating the expression *Anty talig,*

This is what my husband did. He uttered the words, and in so doing, he decided my fate. I was helpless. I couldn't do anything. We were divorced the moment he spoke the words. And when I received the letter from the court, I knew that was it.

To this day, there has been no communication between my ex-husband and our two sons. What bothers me the most is that my husband did not apply for passports for our sons. By law, the children must take the nationality of the father. In my country, I cannot apply for passports or nationalities for my children because only the father, not the mother, can give nationalities in the Gulf Cooperation Council countries.[3]

I cannot send my sons to schools, because schools will not accept them. They have no citizenship, no passports, no identification cards. I cannot tell you how difficult it is to get medical services, education, and basic things to live. I am heartbroken for my sons and I cannot do anything about it.

I worry every time they are sick, because I cannot take them to

which translates to "You are divorced." This is a right given to a man which he may exercise at his sole discretion. A man does not have to have reasons to do so, and for the divorce to occur he needs to simply confirm that he has divorced the woman by extracting a divorce paper from the Sharia courts. Conversely, a woman must file a case before the Sharia courts to get a divorce. Most Sharia courts are reluctant to grant a woman a divorce easily and instead suggest mediation. If a woman does not sufficiently prove that she was abused, she must offer her husband money to get the divorce. Usually, the money paid by the women is the amount of dowry paid to her upon marriage.

3   All GCC countries do not allow women to pass their nationality to their children. All children are given the nationality of their father. It is worth noting that although the GCC countries have signed and ratified the Convention for the Elimination of All Forms of Discrimination against Women (CEDAW), they have made reservations against the article that allows a woman to pass her nationality to her children.

the government hospital, and I cannot afford private healthcare.

We live every day in fear and pain.

Is there any fate worse than a mother afraid for the lives of her sons?

I try to focus on being positive and remind myself that I am safe. At least I am no longer with a man who hurts me. I will persevere. My children will persevere, somehow. I have read dozens of books about abuse, and I understand better now how trauma works in our brains and bodies. I try not to hate myself, and I fight against the pervasive shame I have carried with me for so long. I have finally begun the long process of recovering my self-worth.

Is there any fate worse than a mother afraid for the lives of her sons?

Above all else, I am a mother. And I will fight for my sons until my dying breath.

Sincerely,
The GCC Mother

P.S.

The GCC Mother's story breaks my heart. It also speaks to the inherent injustices of the legal system in this part of the world. If a male citizen of the Gulf Cooperation Council marries a foreigner, his children immediately receive citizenship at birth. Why are Gulf Arab women not granted the same privilege? Why can't a mother who is a natural citizen of a country not give her children her citizenship?

In most countries around the globe, this disparity does not exist. In the Western world, there would be outrage if a mother gave birth to a child in her own country and was told they did not have citizenship, that they could not have passports, that she could not send her sons or daughters to school or take them to the hospital.

And yet, in most of the Arab world, lawmakers refuse to withdraw the reservations they made to the CEDAW that would change these laws. They allow mothers to be stripped of these basic rights. It is Arab women who are birthing the next generation. It is Arab mothers who have the power and grace to raise their children to be conscientious citizens who give back to their communities and countries. And yet because of the laws, those children may never be citizens at all.

Women make up more than 50 percent of the population. We are no longer considered the weaker and submissive gender. The world needs us to survive—so grant us rights, and respect them.

The Gulf Businesswoman

I ENTERED A BEAUTIFUL HOUSE *and met an elegant woman in her sixties, thick black hair drawn back into a bun, her face welcoming and beautiful. She was dressed in a long skirt and kaftan, her jewelry impeccable. She exuded class.*

I considered myself lucky to be in her stunning home. I knew a good bit about her: she belonged to one of the most prominent and influential business families in the Gulf.

We kissed on the cheek the traditional Arabic way.

"Tell me," I said. "Why do you want to do this interview?"

The Gulf Businesswoman held my hand while we sat next to each other. She was surrounded by so many beautiful things, yet I saw sadness in her eyes.

"All throughout my life," she told me, "I have felt a sense of injustice.

My rights have been taken away from me. For as long as I can remember, I have been plagued by the same question: was I let down by my father, or by the system?"

She began to tell me her story. In 1954, her father passed away suddenly in his sleep at a young age …

I was one and a half years old when my father passed away. I never knew him, but I always heard that he was hardworking and brought many ventures into the company. I was the youngest of six girls, and I grew up hearing from an early age that my father wanted all his daughters to study abroad. At the time, this was unique. My father was a forward-thinking man who had big ambitions and big dreams to match.

I grew up in a house with a loving mother and loving sisters. Everyone adored my mother—she was generous, witty, and intelligent, even if she couldn't read or write. Our house was the house that everyone congregated to. In this day and age, you might say it had an amazing energy. At the time, all I knew was that my mother drew everyone in. Once my five older sisters began to have children, they would beg to come to see their grandmother, to listen to her laugh and hear her stories. She was the favorite mother and grandmother to all.

To this day, my sisters and I have a unique relationship. My mother united us all with love and respect; she was a unique angel who will always be remembered. She gave us formidable advice—except about one thing. She always told us never to question our brothers.

"They are good boys," she said, "who will always care for you and protect you. You must not question them."

At the time, I agreed. My brothers were polite, though by today's standards, they would be considered dictatorial. They approved or disapproved everything in their sisters' lives before marriage. Anything we wanted to do, we had to obtain their approval.

Fortunately, my brothers honored our father's wish that all of his daughters study abroad. I went to university in Kuwait, and after I returned, I met a gentleman from another well-recognized business family. We were married soon after.

My husband was wonderful to me. He treated me like a queen. He encouraged me to work and move forward in life, to make my own decisions and accept the outcomes, whether good or bad.

I had a daughter and sons, and I was happily surprised when my husband treated our daughter as an equal. He never enforced limitations on her or rules that were different than those he enforced on our sons—something I knew was unique in our region, because I would hear other women speak of how differently their husbands treated their daughters versus their sons. Including my own sisters. To this day, my daughter is equal to my sons regarding ownership of shares and cash.

I wish I could say the same had been true in my own life.

While my sisters and I were growing up, we were told that, before our father's unfortunate early death, he had relinquished all our rights in the company to our brothers. We never understood how that could be possible for such a forward-thinking man. Our father wanted us to study abroad and see the world. Why would he treat us differently when it came to the family business? It simply didn't add up.

Islamic law was supposed to protect us. But our mother always told us not to question our brothers. So we did not.

Our brothers and male cousins persuaded us to sign over a small number of land deeds to our family: a fraction of our father's wealth. We received a nominal amount of cash for the sale of the lands. At the time, we took it in good faith, but there was always a question in the back of all our minds. When one of us *did* make an inquiry or raise a concern, we were always told adamantly: "You are married to a wealthy man! So why question?"

Decades passed. I witnessed the hypocrisy that my brothers and their children lived through. My sisters felt cheated more and more, and the lies that they had been told were becoming obvious. These men never had our best interests at heart.

The sense of injustice never left me. It was not about the money. It was that my own family betrayed my trust.

I want to tell my story because it is the story of so many women. It is the story of injustice to daughters, sisters, and wives. I do not want future women to fall into the same trap that we fell into, to agree to anything less than they deserve. The same things are happening today that happened decades ago. We cannot allow this to continue.

I do not want future women to fall into the same trap that we fell into, to agree to anything less than they deserve.

How can we as women stay silent? We are all sisters, mothers, and daughters. No one has a right to take our rights away. We cannot and should not continue to be the silent, submissive gender. We have rights—and we must demand more.

Sincerely,
The Gulf Businesswoman

P.S.

Unfortunately, this story is not uncommon. Many times, at the end of their father's life, brothers can pressure their sisters to sign documents that force them to give up their shares in the family business. They are able to do this because women don't carry their father's name through their children.

Here in the Arab world, children do not carry the name of their grandfather on their mother's side; the line of lineage changes. So in many substantial merchant families, brothers or fathers use that argument to ask the daughters to leave the company by paying them a fraction of what they would be worth. The argument tends to be that, as women, we are overly emotional and can be heavily influenced by our husbands. As if the opposite is not true!

This has repeatedly happened to renowned families and large conglomerates in the Arab business world, which is why I wanted to include the Gulf Businesswoman's story in this book. As women, we are coerced or forced to be submissive to a brother or a husband. Kicking the sisters out at the end of the father's life is more common than uncommon. Many women have been forced to stay silent, but when this story comes out, I feel they will begin to speak their truth.

It is always about lineage and the pedigree of the man in the family carrying the father's name through his children, and the daughter's children carry another man's name. So strange that in this day and age we still think this way. I feel the men are selfishly using any excuse to take over their sisters' rights. They argue that the sisters' husbands will be greedy and a bad influence. Yet, from what I have seen in life, the opposite is just as true: the brothers' wives heavily influence them.

Now the men who have unjustly treated their sisters are in the position of having daughters. The question is: How will they treat their daughters? In some cases, they know what they or their fathers have done, so they have stipulated that their daughters should have board rights! So strange after their sisters were denied those rights. But looking forward, maybe this is the change we are looking for.

The majority of businesses in this part of the world are family businesses. So what is the solution to this issue? I must admit that this generation is always attending family business seminars out of the country with reputable international educational schools. Most are in the process of writing the family constitution. The question lies in how they will treat their sisters and daughters. My hope is that, since we are educated just like our brothers—if not more highly educated—we should consider all offspring as individuals. In other words, we should be judged by merit. The family members who are most capable should be rewarded, regardless of gender.

Times are changing. The court system is willing to hear our cases— they are required to now, a consequence of the many changes our leaders have instituted. Our present leaders, whether in the Kingdom of Bahrain, the Kingdom of Saudi Arabia, or the United Arab Emirates, have made gigantic leaps to empower women. They are the disruption we need.

Now we must believe in ourselves. We have to believe we have the rights and capabilities—and then keep up the fight for those rights. I understand this is the beginning. But all stories start at the beginning. I hope the Gulf Businesswoman's story shows there is light at the end of the tunnel and encourages other Arab women to step forward.

We can all hope for beautiful endings. But we must work to achieve them.

The Kuwaiti Influencer

I MET UP WITH THE KUWAITI INFLUENCER *at a restaurant renowned for its lavish breakfast buffet. She was well dressed, with a cute, charming smile and dark, curly hair framing her face. She spoke perfect English, and her voice had a natural warmth and grace.*

"I try to eat well," she explained, as she returned from the buffet with a plate of fresh fruit. "I feel so much better when I do."

The Kuwaiti Influencer was confident, bold without being brash—a trait I had noticed and admired in many of the Kuwaiti women I'd met.

"Are you from Kuwait originally?" I asked.

"Yes. But my husband and I are actually talking about leaving."

"You've been here your whole life?"

She nodded. "My whole life."

"That's a big deal, then."

"Honestly, we've been talking about moving for a while, even before this whole drama happened."

She let out a big sigh—and set her plate of fruit aside.

I never thought I'd grow up to be a healer. But I've always been interested in meditation. Even as a young girl, I was fascinated by the story of Prophet Mohammed (God bless his soul) going into the cave in Huraa to retreat from the world. What did he do in there, I wondered? The Quran talks about how we should look at the mountains and meditate on creation, but no one explained to me how to meditate, or what meditation even was.

Years later, I was studying biomedical engineering at an American university. I faced many challenges in my studies and relationships. Something in me knew I needed to make a change. In the midst of that dark place, I found a meditation center next to my house.

The first time I meditated was a transformative moment in my life. My worries, fear, and depression began to subside as I learned how to connect with my inner power and with God.

I eventually found my way to Pranic Healing, a highly evolved and tested system of energy medicine. Prana is a Sanskrit word that means "life force." Prana can balance, harmonize, and transform the body's energy processes. This invisible vital energy keeps us alive and helps us maintain a state of good health.

I travelled to train in this technique. I started giving away free Pranic Healing sessions from my home to anyone who needed them. The results were amazing. After only a half-hour treatment, people began to experience a tremendous amount of peace and calm. Even their pains and aches ebbed away.

I got so busy with my clients that I decided to quit my job at a local hospital and become a full-time healer. The next step was to become a teacher, speaking about many issues related to bodies and healing. I wanted to share my knowledge to teach people how to heal themselves.

I suppose you could say that's where the trouble started.

As a part of my practice as an energy healer, I do live meditations on YouTube. A while back, a lady who's well known as a food blogger commented on one of my videos, saying nasty things about me as a person. Needless to say, I was upset.

I tracked down her number and gave her a call.

"Why are you saying these things?" I asked.

To my surprise, she said she was sorry. I asked her to apologize publicly and she agreed. The video went viral.

The blogger explained to me that she had a relative who wrote a book against energy healing, and it was this woman who told her to make those comments on my video. She sent me her relative's contact information, and we ended up exchanging phone calls, back and forth, as she tried relentlessly to convince me her way was right. It was so exhausting. Finally I said, "You know what? We will never agree. Goodbye."

She took it personally—and became even more upset. That interaction would come back to haunt me, based on what happened next.

Last year I started a campaign about sex education. My mother and I were on a train when I had the idea. We were coming back from a trip to Vienna, and I was feeling inspired by how open-minded and liberated Viennese women were in talking about these things.

I told my mother, "I'm fed up with being silent. I want to talk about it."

She said, "Go ahead."

I posted my first post with her blessing. My husband was very supportive too. In Kuwait sex is a very controversial subject, but I felt—still feel—that it's important. I wanted to talk about how sex as we see it portrayed in the movies is not real. I went deeper into talking about a woman's vagina and clitoris. It wasn't sensationalist. It was all very scientific.

In Kuwait sex is a very controversial subject, but I felt—still feel—that it's important.

I didn't do YouTube videos, but I would post on social media. I would put it up on my Instagram, then remove the post, just on the off chance that someone might take legal action against me. Some men got very offended, as I suspected they might. But that was all right. I wasn't doing this for them.

In one post, I wrote in Arabic, "My vagina …" then encouraged my followers to fill in the blank, because I wanted women to think positively about their vaginas. In another post, I talked about how through sexuality we can connect with God. I said it in a polite way, not quite so directly. I called it "spiritual sex."

I was posting every day. And the amount of feedback I got was overwhelmingly positive. Women were so happy I was talking about these subjects. They found my words healing, and they were grateful I was giving them a forum for discussion. My follower count increased dramatically.

But I was still being safe. Or so I thought. I'd leave each post up for a few minutes or hours, then hit delete. The problem was that my Instagram account is linked to my Twitter. On the day I posted about spiritual sex, I removed it from my Instagram … but forgot to do the same on Twitter.

The angry woman was lurking in the wings, of course. Waiting for me to mess up. She saw the tweets and took screenshots.

The next day, I got a phone call from the Kuwaiti police. They said I needed to come down to the station. The woman had retained a lawyer—and the lawyer filed a cybercriminal evidence charge against me. They also filed a second charge, violation of public decency, because they claimed I had said blasphemous things against God.

Of course I tried to explain that I wasn't blaspheming God. If anything, I was doing the opposite: talking about spiritual sex as a way to have a real and vibrant relationship with God. But as you might expect, my explanation fell on deaf ears.

And then I lawyered up.

✢   ✢   ✢

While they were doing the integrity interrogation, both my husband and my lawyer were with me. My lawyer kept confirming that it was okay, nothing would happen. She told me the maximum penalty was fifty Kuwaiti dinars (KWD), which is not so much.

"That's it," she said. "You'll pay the fine and you'll just go home."

"Will I go to jail for this?"

"No way," she said. She was so relaxed and laid-back. I believed her.

But the process took longer and longer. Then they came back and told me they were taking me to another place. I was shocked. I had no idea what was happening. My lawyer's face went bright red. My husband was getting panicky.

They started calling people, but it was already too late.

The police took me away, and I spent the night in jail.

The most interesting part was who was with me in detention. They were all women with "sex issues." One woman got pregnant out of wedlock, which in Kuwait is a crime. She didn't know who the father was. She kept giving names, and the police brought in man after man, but each one denied getting her pregnant.

Another woman had been put in detention for cheating on her husband. She told me she'd been asking for a divorce for a really long time, and her husband started to doubt she was faithful. So he followed her. He found her sitting with another man in his apartment. That was all it took.

Some women were there on prostitution charges. Many had come to Kuwait as maids from Madagascar and other parts of Africa. They'd been in detention for a really long time, some as long as three weeks. Even jail is better equipped than a detention center! In detention, you don't have a bed. You sleep on the floor and you all share one toilet. No shower, no sink. Imagine living in those conditions for three weeks.

At a certain point, my lawyer and husband called so many people they were able to move me into a VIP room. I got a bed and my own toilet. My husband brought me a pillow, my pajamas, a toothbrush, and a book, which was amazing.

But I did spend the night in jail.

Leaving the next day was not easy. They wanted me to stay longer, but because I was still breastfeeding my son, they let me out on a bail of five hundred KWD. It was a lot of money, especially for a minor Instagram post. Frankly, I had posted far more inflammatory things on social media! Talking about masturbation and all kinds of sexual topics that in Kuwait are seen as taboo.

Afterward, the police told me, "We're so sorry." My father has a lot of connections, and once he got involved, things escalated quickly. Of course he wished I hadn't talked about sex so publicly. Imagine the embarrassment, him calling everybody he knew to get me out, and them all wanting to know, "What did she do?"

After months of going through all the legal processes, the verdict came. The cybercriminal evidence case disappeared because one of my lawyers asked them to drop the charges, and they did. For the public decency case, I was charged as guilty, but without being penalized.

All my posts on social media are gone now, of course.

Delete, delete, delete.

People ask me if, after my experience, I've stopped talking about sex. Absolutely not. I no longer do it on social media—but I will never stop. This is a passion of mine. And after spending a night in jail with my cellmates, I realized just how important the conversation around sex is in the Arabic world. It gave me even *more* of a passion to continue this work.

I started by helping the women in jail. One of my very good friends is the granddaughter of the Emir of Kuwait. She works a lot with social services, so I contacted her. She intervened and got the pregnant woman I met in jail a lawyer. She was able to immediately relocate the women who'd spent three weeks in detention. So I felt there was a lot of good that came out of it.

Now I offer private sessions. I travel and teach in different countries. People ask me to come into their homes and talk about these issues. Sometimes twenty or thirty women will gather together in the same room, often from the most conservative countries, and ask me questions they've never before been able to ask.

I want women to be able to talk. Just talk. There is so much we're still learning. This is the sort of knowledge I believe should be shared. This is all a part of healing. We must heal both our bodies and our minds.

Sincerely,
The Kuwaiti Influencer

P.S.

I think a lot of changes are coming. As we continue to grow and expand the Arab world, why aren't we growing and expanding our legal foundation? We can't live in buildings that have the infrastructure of twenty-first century but cling to goals from the seventh century. How is it we have the world's most beautiful skyscrapers, but talking about sex is still largely uncommon and not readily encouraged?

We've used the latest technology to build these buildings—we're constantly using new and more advanced technologies. We are known for our airports and flights, which are staffed by female flight attendants who are modernly dressed. We serve alcohol on these flights. Why are these behaviors—dressing as one pleases, imbibing at our leisure—okay in the air, but not on the land? Why are these things acceptable—why is our mindset so modern in this way—but not when it comes to a woman speaking her mind?

A woman can be educated, she can be a productive and successful member of society, but she will never live at her best until we change legislation.

There are controversial subjects in this book. Not everyone will agree with the Kuwaiti Influencer. Some will say, "How dare you?" But I think the majority will say they don't want to live a life where, if an unmarried woman gets pregnant, she goes straight to jail.

If people want to live in that world, they can stay in that world. Don't build buildings. Stay in the desert.

But we don't want to stay in the desert. Enough is enough.

The GCC Shadows

AS I WAS WRITING THIS BOOK, *I was privileged to meet an abundance of women who have faced challenges and adversity with strength and grace. I met businesswomen, artists, politicians, journalists, healers, housewives, influencers, media icons, and more. These women were also wives, mothers, daughters, sisters, and friends. They told me their stories in restaurants and cafes, offices and conference rooms. Some even came to my home.*

But in addition to the prominent women who told me their stories, there were other women who were more difficult to access because of their circumstances. Sadly, they often cannot raise their voices, either because they are in dangerous situations or because they do not have the resources or support.

At the end of this book, you'll find a letter written by my daughter, Lara. One thing from Lara's letter that has stayed with me is when she thanked me for "giving women the opportunity to share their stories, women who otherwise would just be shadows." I was touched by Lara's words. It was important to me to give the shadow woman a chance to speak about what she goes through. And while one book cannot change legislation, I believe it can spark a conversation it is time we had.

The following three women are represented by a lawyer working pro bono to help the less fortunate, Aysha Abdulla Mutaywea of Mena Chambers law firm. She not only helped supply the legal background footnoted throughout this book, but she also graciously facilitated the conversations with the three women featured in this letter with me. I have changed their names to protect them.

Um[4] Ali is a housewife who was been struggling in her marriage since its inception. She is a mother of four who suffered emotional, psychological, financial, and physical abuse at the hands of her husband. The kind of abuse she went through is shocking and heartbreaking. Not long after their marriage, her husband suggested that she do her part and try to earn money. He told her that she should sleep with other men to get money.

Bewildered and shocked, she gathered herself and reported this to the police. But the police did nothing. They told her that he was probably just angry and didn't mean it and that no harm had actually come to her. She told them she felt unsafe and didn't want to go back home, but since he was her husband and no actual crime had been committed, nothing was to be done, they said. They asked her to go home.

She lived in fear and shame, worried that one day he might

---

4   In Arabic, *Um* is used as an honorific in place of a woman's name, and means "Mother of." The name that follows *Um* is the name of the woman's son or daughter.

actually force her to sleep with other men to get money. The situation was unbearable, and with the increasing tension, life was unbearable. Her husband verbally divorced her several times, but he refused to go to court to get the divorce paper. According to Islamic scripture, if a man verbally states the term *anty talig*, then the divorce occurs. Once this happens, a couple should not be living together. But he had refused to finalize it, and she was stuck in limbo.

Finally, she decided to file an application for official divorce from the court.

But when the case was heard before the judge, the husband denied that he had divorced her. This would mean months of

The situation was unbearable, and with the increasing tension, life was unbearable.

fighting the case in court since the judge continued to request that she reconcile with her husband.

Meanwhile, the violence was escalating. One day, she could not bear the abuse anymore and decided to leave the house. All she wanted was to feel safe and not worry about when she was going to get another beating.

At the time, the divorce case was still being heard before the court. When she left her house, as she feared for her safety, her husband reported her leaving to the court and asked the judge to order her to return. Um Ali explained that the only reason she left home was that she was being abused and did not feel safe. Nevertheless, the judge ordered her to "return obediently to her marital home," otherwise she would lose any possibility of child custody, financial support, or alimony and would be declared *nashiz* (an Islamic term which means disobedient wife).[5]

---

5   In Sharia law, a woman is required to live either in her husband's house or her

In court her husband accused her of adultery and prostitution. Until today, and after many months of starting this battle to set herself free, Um Ali has been unable to get her divorce due to her husband's manipulative efforts in court. Her husband's false accusations have interfered with her battle to receive full custody of her children.

Um Mohammed is a mother of five and a wife of an abusive husband. Her marriage of twenty-two years has been filled with insults, threats, and beatings.[6] He would also take her salary every month, leaving her with no money at all.[7] He would not just abuse her but his children too. Everyone was petrified at home, and she felt helpless.

When she mustered the strength and courage to raise complaints against her husband with the police, she was ignored. She suspected this was due to the fact that her husband was a policeman. Every time she would complain, the police would contact her husband, who would arrive and take her right back home, and the beating would get worse.[8]

---

father's home. *Nashiz* is a term that refers to a woman who has "disobeyed her husband" by refusing to share his bed or leaving the marital home without the permission of the husband. The result of the declaration of *nashiz* is that the woman loses custody of her children and alimony. In some countries, if a man reports his wife as *nashiz* (i.e., not living with him or having left the house without his permission), the wife is made to return to the marital house by force.

6　Although some GCC countries have domestic abuse laws, they are not enforced effectively and, more often than not, the abused woman is forced to return to her husband's home.

7　In a lot of domestic abuse cases, husbands will not allow their wives to work, or as in Um Mohammed's case, will take their wife's salary for themselves if their wife does work. For this reason, the wife has no source of income and no financial independence, which makes it difficult for the woman to leave the abusive husband.

8　Most abused women interviewed were married to policemen or soldiers. In

Desperate to escape her broken home, she decided to leave the house and sought refuge in a women's shelter. She ended up moving from one shelter to another—shelters could not house abused women for a long period of time, so she ended up overstaying and was forced to leave.[9] Sadly, she could not bring her sons to the shelter, because the shelter did not accept boys above the age of twelve.

Um Mohammed battled tirelessly in family court to get a divorce and custody of her children.[10] She wants to become an independent woman free from her husband's control. She struggles to this day, unsure of her fate and what will become of her children, who have been left with their abusive father.[11]

Um Ebrahim is a mother of four and is married to an abusive man. Her husband holds a GCC country passport. The cycle of abuse began as soon as they got married. He would abuse her with every pregnancy. There were many times when he would physically hit

---

these instances, the abusers have access to weapons and are prone to physical and sexual violence.

9   Not all GCC countries have women's shelters, and the ones that do have restrictions such as not providing a shelter if the woman does not file a police report. Most shelters will not allow a woman to bring her sons with her to the shelter, since it is a place for women only.

10   Family courts take many months, if not years, to decide on cases. Most of the time, the court will try to push the couple to reconcile their differences and remain married. It is very easy for abusive husbands to prolong cases filed by abused women and women asking for divorce. If the husband or the abuser doesn't appear in court, the court will keep delaying the case until he appears. In most cases, divorce is refused on "lack of sufficient grounds" and the woman must go back to her marital home.

11   Although some countries have child protection services, the abused women report that these services are not taken seriously and most of the time nothing is done. It is very rare that the courts would intervene and take children away from a parent in any case.

her in the stomach during her pregnancy, but she bore the pain in silence. She felt she must bear it to avoid social stigma. Divorce is not encouraged, and she would bear the shame of it if it happened. There was no escape.

Finally, her husband decided to leave, but he refused to divorce her and to get passports for his children. He disappeared, leaving her tied to him and leaving his children to live in Bahrain with no recorded identities.[12]

It is Bahraini law (pursuant to the Convention on the Elimination of All Forms of Discrimination against Women, known as CEDAW) that a Bahraini woman may not pass her nationality to her children. In fact, Um Ebrahim attempted to get citizenship for her children, but her plea has gone unheard. The reason for this is that there is no law to grant her the right to pass her nationality to her children.

As a result of bearing no identity, it was a struggle to have her children admitted to schools and universities. They could not qualify for any support or grants. Basic things like state-funded healthcare were not granted to her children, as they did not have Bahrain passports.

Um Ebrahim's sons have never left the country, because they don't have passports. Um Ebrahim dreams of a day when she can pass her nationality to her children and take them out of the country for the first time in their lives.

---

12 In Sharia law, a man can be married to four women at the same time. Women can be married to one man at a time. However, a woman is unable to remarry if she is not legally divorced from her husband. In many cases, a husband will refuse to divorce his wife so that she is unable to remarry or be single.

P.S.

In 1979, the United Nations General Assembly adopted the international CEDAW. It is considered an international bill of rights for women, comprised of a preamble and thirty articles that clearly define what constitutes discrimination against women and lay out an agenda for national action to end such discrimination.

Most notably, the GCC Countries and most Arab countries have declined to accept Article 9 of the CEDAW, which states that "States Parties shall grant women equal rights with men with respect to the nationality of their children."

At the time of this writing, more than forty years after the UN adopted the convention, Arab countries have made reservations to articles 2, 9.2, 15.4, 16, and 29 which, respectively, concern issuing regulations that ensure equal rights to men and women, women passing nationality to their children, the freedom to choose a residence, equal rights in marriage and dissolution of marriage, and the ability to settle disputes before the international court of justice.

The Arabic Dad

I WAS AT AN INVESTMENT CONFERENCE *in the region. The atmosphere was dynamic and exciting, full of investment bankers and dignitaries from all over the world.*

When I mentioned I was writing this book, people started coming up to me at lunch, expressing their interest and support for this project. I have to say, I was pleasantly surprised. I expected to encounter men who were not happy, individuals who would say, "But why? Why would you frame our world negatively to the West?" I was ready to defend myself, to explain that I had no intention of framing our world negatively. I only want to give other Arab women a chance to speak.

But in fact, the opposite happened. The support and interest I received from these men was astounding. During our breaks between sessions, we usually stood in the hallway networking with other delegates, our nametags prominently exposed. We typically discussed what line of business we were in and what we thought of the last session we had attended. This time, the subject of my book inevitably came up—and the group grew larger. The interest from both foreigners and locals was flabbergasting.

The more conservative gentlemen listened quietly, then recited how religion had given women rights. This was true centuries ago, and we are blessed. I gently suggested that life had evolved, and we must continue to evolve with utmost respect to our beautiful religion.

By the time dinner rolled around, I had learned that men were also interested in this topic, far more than I had assumed. I felt they, too, wanted to see change for their daughters, for the future generation. After dinner I went back to my hotel. As I was turning on the television, I heard a noise. Someone had slipped a letter under the door. On the front of the envelope, they had written my name.

I had no idea what to expect. Was someone going to berate me for writing my book? Had I angered or offended one of the men at the conference, and he had chosen to chastise me in a private letter rather than calling me out in public?

But when I opened the envelope, I found none of those things. Instead I found a letter from a father written to his daughter. The letter was not signed with a name. Just "Dad." Did I know the writer? Maybe, maybe not. But this father wanted to be heard.

To My Darling Girl:

I can't believe you've fled the nest already. I remember the day I held both of your tiny feet in the palm of one of my hands. Your journey in our world had just started. It was clear to me then that your life force was so strong. Large brown eyes observing every nuance around them. Taking it all in. Wanting more every second. All of that has not changed now that you're an amazing young woman of eighteen springs.

What does an Arab father tell his cherished daughter as she departs? Do I remind you of the dangers of living in the West? The temptations of life? To watch out for men? Be afraid of consequences? Protect your virginity and innocence?

I would never say any of these things, my baby. I would tell you that your virtue is not physical. It is in the way you carry yourself. It should be consistent with the essence of who you are. The farther away you are from yourself, no matter which direction, the farther you are from your real virtue. It is not a hymen. Our society is so farcical: it seems this standard applies only to girls. Arab boys seem to be excluded. We raised you and your brother under the same standard. I hope that you will remember us well, both of you.

Do I tell you to pray? To fear God? I would tell you not to fear anyone or anything. No god wants to be feared. Besides, God is within you, closer than your veins. You want to speak to him and seek guidance? Speak to him within. There you will find answers to your questions. I want you to think critically, love unconditionally, live fully, and smile, smile, smile … because our life is just a collection of moments. Make each one count.

What about money and material possessions? "Marry well," some may say. I would ask you to hold off on that venture till you know who you are. Till you've discovered the woman you aspire to be. Only you know what it will take to make you happy. Do not give that right to anyone else in your life. For life is the choices you make. I hope that you make the choices that ensure you grow as a person. To recognize your role as a steward for the planet on which we live. To fill your heart with love for

Only you know what it will take to make you happy. Do not give that right to anyone else in your life.

everything living. Because being alive is so damned precious. That is the true nature of our humanity.

Love for eternity,
Dad

P.S.

Originally I was not going to have any letters from men in this book. The subtitle is, after all, "Letters from Arab Women." But the Arabic Dad's words touched me.

The more men I spoke to about these issues, the more I realized that many Arabic fathers are facing similar dilemmas—far more than I assumed. How should they raise their daughters to be strong and independent and to inherit this new world? In family business, some men are worried about their daughters. Will their brothers take care of them? Who will protect them? Of course, what these men often fail to realize is that if they empower their daughters and treat them all equally, then they will have the ability to protect themselves.

The GCC Free Spirit

I WAS HAVING BREAKFAST with an American friend who'd come for a visit. Together we sat in the hotel restaurant, windows on all sides, looking down on the city hurtling past below. We'd come to the hotel to meet with the GCC Free Spirit.

When we saw her walking toward us, my friend turned to me and said quietly, "She's completely covered. I didn't expect a woman wearing a hijab would be able to speak openly about these subjects for the book."

I smiled at my friend. "This is the most incorrect perception the West has of women who are covered. Being modest and conservative does not mean you have to be completely submissive. These women have opinions and character, just the same as any woman in the West. They've simply chosen to cover their hair and dress in a more conservative fashion because of their beliefs."

"You're right," my friend admitted. "This is something we Westerners have trouble understanding. I think many of us often see a woman in *a hijab or abaya and have a knee-jerk reaction of, 'She's being controlled or abused.'"*

I shook my head. "The scarf covering their hair does not signify a helpless woman—it's the opposite. All women should have the same respect and rights. Our law system does not separate or discriminate between color or covered."

We welcomed the GCC Free Spirit to our table and ordered breakfast. My American friend leaned in, listening attentively as this woman's remarkable story began to unfold.

I am a Bedoon. You might hear this and think "Bedouin," but it is not the same. The word *Bedouin* comes from the word *nomad*, and although some Bedoons are of Bedouin origin, most of us have been settled in urban centers for centuries. We have never lived a nomadic life.

In Arabic we have an expression: *bedoon jinsiyya*. In English, this translates roughly to "without nationality" or "without citizenship."

That is what it means to be Bedoon. To have the constant knowledge inside you that your identity, your truth, your very *being* could be erased at any time.

In some ways, it might sound freeing. But of course, when you are talking about a group of people stripped of even their most basic rights, freedom is not the word I would use.

I think a lot about freedom. What it means to have it—and how it feels to have it taken away.

For Bedoons, our chief loyalty is to our tribe. We live in countries that actively discriminate against us. We have been refused employment and restricted in where we can live. Our children have been denied education. We are denied citizenship and essentially rendered stateless. We live in the wealthiest countries in the world, but we do so in a constant state of fear: we know that at any moment we could be arrested or deported. We've seen it happen to people we love.

But we do not survive on fear alone. There is great strength and resilience in the Bedoon community, and more diversity than you might think. There are Southern Bedoons. There are Northern Bedoons. Even within one tribe, we have different traditions.

We are, in many ways, conservative. As women, we cover ourselves. But we women also study to be doctors and engineers. My sister is an electrical engineer. Perhaps because we have been oppressed for so long, there's also a rich culture of activism, with different groups championing different rights. We know how to fight for the things we want.

Perhaps this is why a part of me was always a free spirit. Both an instinct true to my Bedoon upbringing, and at the same time, an impulse that compelled me to not let my freedom be taken from me.

Not so long ago, Bedoon women married in high school, around age sixteen or seventeen. These days, you marry once you've finished high school.

I got married at eighteen.

My husband was not a bad man. But I did not want to be married to him. I hadn't been given a choice: my parents chose him and married the two of us, because that was what was done in our Bedoon community. My husband was only two years older, hardworking and respectful. My family felt it was a good match.

But I never wanted it. And not because I wanted to run off to America or rebel in any of the ways we see in the movies. I wasn't opposed to the idea of a husband—just not then. And not *him*.

So I asked him for a divorce. He thought I was kidding. I asked him again. And again. And again.

I really think he thought, "Oh, she's young. She doesn't get it. She'll come around." Though he was only twenty! He just didn't understand that I didn't want him.

I tried to commit suicide.

He still didn't get it.

For a full year, I told him, "Give me a divorce. Give me a divorce." He still didn't listen.

So I cheated on him.

It wasn't the path I would have chosen—if I'd been able to find any other path. The Bedoons have our own courts and legal system, and I couldn't appeal to them. I couldn't ask my family for help, because they wouldn't hear it. Among the Bedoons, a divorce is not easy to attain.

So after months of begging my husband for a divorce, I made the painful decision to be discovered with another man. It was the only way for him to fully understand that I didn't want to be married.

And it worked: he gave me the divorce.

But it was a huge scandal for my family. They locked me at home for almost a year. They abandoned me. I wasn't able to go to college anymore. I had to make many sacrifices, give up things I loved.

At the time, my mother stood by my father. Now she understands what they did was wrong. But the scandal was very bad, and I do pity them for how much my choice exploded their lives. It was simply the only way I knew how to survive.

At nineteen, I got my divorce.

I have five children now, with my second husband. We live in a lovely home. I feel very fulfilled as a wife and mother.

To this day, I don't hate my first husband. He still visits my family. I know the culture itself was to blame.

And I know the culture is changing. Slowly. Steadily. I see the work other Bedoon activists are doing, raising their voices to demand better laws and better cultural understanding. If a woman wants a divorce, she should not have to cheat on her husband to obtain it. There need to be support systems in place, clear and empowering paths. She shouldn't have to risk destroying her family to feel happy and free.

I don't think any woman can say she's forced to stay in a relationship unless she has a gun pointed to her head. If you persist, you *can* find a way out. It was very hard for me to get a divorce, but I did it.

I knew what freedom looked like.

I did what I had to do to make it mine.

Sincerely,
The GCC Free Spirit

P.S.

Suffice it to say, after the GCC Free Spirit's story was finished, my American friend was pleasantly surprised. "What a strong and enterprising woman!" she said, as we stepped out of the hotel and into the morning sun.

The strength of a woman has nothing to do with whether or not she chooses to cover her hair. There is no correlation. Wearing a hijab (headscarf) does not mean a woman is submissive. I have friends who wear it, and it's perfectly normal. There are many different reasons a woman might wear one—it could be religion, family influence, cultural influence. But it does not take away her strength.

I think many people in the Western world believe that if a woman has her hair covered, she is a very submissive woman. That really couldn't be further from the truth. It is a choice she makes. What's nice about our society is that we respect the GCC Free Spirit's choice, just as we also respect my choice to not be covered.

The Syrian Refugee

ONE DAY I WENT ON MY USUAL TRIPS *to the refugee camps and to visit with other refugees living in the city. I knocked on a door in the basement of a building, and a woman answered. She let me in and introduced me to her beautiful young daughter and her husband's second wife and two daughters, all lovely and graceful ladies.*

As I was giving her a donation, she held my hand abruptly.

"You know I was like you in my country," she said. "Going house to house and giving to the needy. Now look at me. We fled with nothing but our clothes on our backs."

I will never forget those words. I was like you.

Can this happen to any of us?

The Syrian Refugee was a woman full of pride. But out of necessity she accepted my gift with trembling hands and a bowed head. I could feel her giving up hope. Her pain shone in her eyes, her loss of the will to live.

"Only my daughter Maryam," she whispered in my ear, "keeps me alive."

I live here with my family now. Far away from my homeland that I was forced to leave, running from the hell of war. Searching for the freedom that I never had. Heading to a new life that we knew nothing about. Here I am trying to collect my missing pieces and stand up for the thousandth time.

I am staring at the horizon of the future, Maryam, looking at you playing with the only toy you have. I see you crying when you wish you had toys like the other children have. Every time I try to convince you of what we do have.

The dress that is smaller than your size.

The tattered schoolbooks you must use.

The old bag someone donated.

It is not much, but it is something.

I am here now, waiting for my destiny to have mercy on me.

I am here now, my daughter. I am here with you.

Your father was injured by a sniper. He cannot walk anymore. The pain eats my soul whenever I look at him. He used to be a strong man, full of hopes and dreams. We used to stand up for our ethics and fight for the good life we deserve.

He cannot stand at all anymore. Not for anything. Not even to walk. I cannot find a stable job to live the kind of life I dreamed of for you, Maryam. All of this comes with the unthinkable truth that we have no right to be humans.

I know you remember Syria. You remember the house we lived in, your grandparents' house, the grocery store we used to go to, the small park where you would play. You were a very little girl, and now you are twelve years old. You are growing up right before my eyes. Soon you will be a teenager.

All my dreams fly around your future, education, even your basic needs. You are growing up to be a beautiful girl without any expectations. All my dreams are dreams for you.

All my dreams fly around your future, education, even your basic needs.

I have a bachelor's degree in English literature. I worked in translation, but couldn't get enough money to feed my family. The medicine my husband needs is so expensive, so I'm working with women who are preparing homemade food for families here. The money they pay is not enough, and it's a seasonal job, but still it's better than nothing.

If I were to write a letter to the world, I would ask that they remember the repercussions of war for the innocent.

But this letter is for you, Maryam. In it I will write the words I do not have the strength to say to you.

I love you, sweetheart. I wish I could help more. You must study hard. Wipe up my tears with your education. I want you to slowly work your way out of this life and soar toward success.

I hope we can have a real home again, my love. I hope you can find happiness and wash all this agony and pain away.

I am so exhausted. So tired of being helpless. Though I still have faith in you. You are God's gift to me, despite all the odds. Together we will defeat bad luck and isolation. We will have our new start and our new life.

My little sunshine, you are my most precious treasure. It is the world versus us, but we are fighters. *Survivors.* We will face all the hardships and survive these difficult times. I'll work hard, knock on all doors, and bring you the life you deserve.

You, my little one. You're going to be patient and study hard to guarantee your future.

Here, both of us are going to stand and walk to a new life full of hope and great expectations.

I love you my sweetest daughter, my friend, my companion through this journey.

Maryam, I take refuge in you.

Sincerely,
The Syrian Refugee

P.S.

The conflict in Syria has been ongoing for over eight years. Eight years of innocent deaths. Eight years of mothers crying tears that could fill oceans. Over 8 million Syrians have fled their country to neighboring countries and beyond.

3.5 million to Turkey

2 million to Lebanon

1.5 million to Jordan

1 million to Europe

700,000 to Egypt and Iraq

With time their plight is slowly forgotten, their dreams disintegrating. Mothers' hearts full of sorrow …

How can we try to comprehend how it feels to have to get up and leave your country immediately to save your family? To get up with only the clothes on your back and flee to live in tents? To sleep on the floor not knowing where your next meal might be?

The Saudi
Media Icon

THE SAUDI MEDIA ICON WAS A BEAUTIFUL WOMAN. *She had flawless light-colored skin and soft features. Her emotions were all in her expressions, her hands moving fluidly as her eyes spoke directly to me. She was dressed in a trendy but modest way, her hair covered in a pale hijab.*

When I told her I was curating a collection of letters from Arab women, she jumped in immediately.

"All women have struggles they go through," she said. "We all have multilayered and complex stories. I don't think I've faced exceptional circumstances. The challenges I've come up against are within the norm."

"Do you think it's because you weren't raised here?" I asked. Earlier she'd told me that she grew up in the United States, then Malaysia.

She thought about it for a moment, then replied, "Perhaps. I feel

I don't have the inhibitions I might have had if I'd grown up in Saudi Arabia. I've always asked for my rights without feeling like I was pleading for favors. But that doesn't mean it's always been easy."

I leaned back in my chair, ready to listen.

My mother was from a respected Lebanese family, and my father was from Saudi Arabia. He was well educated, attending an Ivy League university in the United States in the 1950s, which was not common for Saudi men back then.

The importance of education was deeply embedded in my family. I went through the public education system in the US, then went to university at the age of seventeen. Some people called me a prodigy, but I believe it was because I was privileged enough to have lived in three different countries, absorbing three very different cultures: American, Malaysian, and Saudi.

At seventeen, I married a Saudi gentleman by choice. After ten years, we realized our value systems were not the same, so I asked for a divorce. We had two daughters, and I wanted to have a good relationship with their father for their sakes, as well as for mine. We were young when we married, and we grew up together. In essence, we were almost best friends.

But even though we reached an amicable agreement, I still suffered psychologically. No divorce is completely amicable. Legally he has custody of the girls, and he took my passport in the beginning so I wouldn't flee anywhere with them. I decided to remain in Riyadh so their father could see them daily. Even though I had chosen to divorce my husband, I did my best to not damage our daughters. There is a hole in the heart of children of divorce that never completely heals. I hope by making the choices I've made, that hole is much smaller.

I chose not to remarry, primarily because the system was not going to help me. This is yet another example of how a mother sacrifices. Though now that the system has changed, mothers have more rights.

In Saudi, the only job available was teaching at the university. I took it. I was considered something of a rebel at the time—I didn't believe in the existing structures and was always challenging my students.

Then a unique opportunity presented itself. I was invited to be one of the ladies on a talk show, the Arabic equivalent of *The View*. I saw it as a chance to be a pioneer. We had Lebanese, Egyptian, and other Arabic women on television, but not Saudi. I felt it was important to have better Saudi representation in the media, to express our viewpoint, and for others to see a Saudi woman on TV.

I joked with my friends that it was an internal cultural revolution. As a Saudi woman, I was willing to take a chance.

When my career in television began, some conservative women in Saudi did not accept me. They called me *kafara*, which means infidel, a woman of no religion. And yet the Hejazis from the western coast of Saudi Arabia and other Saudi women thought it was wonderful to have a Saudi woman representing them.

I should note that I was not only a Saudi, but also a *muthajba*, meaning I wore the conservative head scarf and modest clothing. I wear this by choice, and I believe in it. It might not be for everyone, but it is for me. I never doubted the concept of wearing a hijab, and I have a strong mindset, so when people respond with judgment or a lack of understanding, I deal with the issues as they arise.

The TV show I was on experienced huge success. It was the number-one talk show for seventeen years, and we received numerous accolades and awards. Sometimes I still reflect on how the administrator at the university told me, "If you take this job, I will fire you."

But I fought back. I said, "You have male lecturers who are not fired for being on television. I should be awarded the same rights." I took a chance—and decided to be a pioneer facing all the consequences, head on. Today I'm very glad I did.

> **I took a chance and decided to be a pioneer facing all the consequences, head on. Today I'm very glad I did.**

I am a survivor. I am always looking for the end game and asking myself, "What outcome do I want to achieve?" I always know what I want out of life. It is my life's work to keep coming back to that life purpose, over and over again.

Sincerely,
The Saudi Media Icon

P.S.

Women like the Saudi Media Icon have experienced great success. It was easy for her to talk about her achievements and accolades—and as she did, I asked about her feelings every step of the way, including how she responded to the impediments on her journey. How did she react to each one? Did she have any regrets?

Compiling the letters for this book has opened my eyes to so many aspects of life as an Arab woman. As I've met a host of lovely, successful letter writers, I've looked for their challenges and how they overcame them against all odds—without realizing that what I was in search for was, in fact, myself! In each woman, I saw a bit of my own story, and as I gave them space to speak their truths, I was forced to examine different layers of my own journey.

I came to realize the questions I was asking the Saudi Media Icon and all of these women were truly for myself. I know how it feels to be in the same echelon of successful women, which means I also know the journey is not easy. Beneath each smile is a deep well of strength and endurance.

Some days, I feel all Arab women need to be awarded with Oscars. We keep working and outperforming to continuously prove ourselves, all with a smile. We are daughters, sisters, wives, and mothers. Each position requires different roles from us, and yet we perform them with aplomb, all the while contributing to the future generation's mentality and attitude.

I remember once at my company, we were called in to an emergency board meeting, in another country, on the same day. The rest of the board were men, so they went home, picked up their pull bags, and proceeded to the airport. I quietly panicked! I was calculating how long it would take me to pass by the nail salon and blow dry my hair, and what suits I needed to pack. This had nothing to do with vanity—it was about trying to look presentable for the right occasions. In this day and age of social media and a camera on everyone's phone, there is added pressure on women, even women CEOs. We don't have to be glamorous, but we have to be presentable if we want to command respect.

The feeling of guilt never seems to leave us. Have we spent enough quality time with our children? Should we work and travel less to be with them more? Some days we are at the office in meetings while our kids are home with fevers. But even amidst the constant guilt, somewhere down the line I realized we needed to take care of ourselves before taking care of others. My children received all the love in the world possible from me, and beautiful quality time I don't think they will ever deny. They have all excelled in their careers or school. But what is most important is that they have respect for everyone around them. The way my sons respect women and their sister makes me emotional and full of pride. Like the Saudi Media Icon, I feel all of us need to find a purpose in life. That purpose, that passion, whatever it may be, will make us happier. The fountain of youth and happiness is within us—we don't need to look elsewhere. Each individual is different, so asking everyone to conform to the same path is impossible. We must all walk different paths to find our own summits.

The GCC Fighter

THE SUSHI RESTAURANT WAS POPULAR, *buzzing with people on a Friday night. I sat at a corner table waiting for the GCC Fighter. I spotted her in the crowd, an attractive woman wearing jeans and an elegant shirt, straight brown hair falling loose around her shoulders.*

I waved her over, then stood and greeted her with a kiss on each cheek. As we sat facing each other, I felt her sadness. But I felt her resilience, too, an underlying layer of strength.

The restaurant was noisy. In between appetizers I sometimes had to ask my questions twice. I learned that she had grown up in a comfortable lifestyle. She'd travelled the world, vacationed in Europe, and studied in the States. After graduating from university in Boston, she secured a great job and launched a promising career. Her professional life couldn't have been going better.

It was her personal life that nearly destroyed her. A battle she's still fighting to this day.

I'd just started working at a telecommunications company. One day a man came up to me. We worked in the same department, though I was in a more senior position.

"I remember you from Boston," he said.

He'd studied in Boston around the same time I had, though we never actually met there—we weren't really in the same crowds. But when he approached me at work, he was super nice and very helpful. He said he didn't have many friends, so I asked if he wanted to grab dinner sometime and offered to introduce him to some of my friends.

And that's where the story started.

At first, things were great. He was open minded, intelligent, funny, generous, kind—and he proposed to me after three days. I was like, "Three days is a bit too quick!"

So we dated for a more reasonable amount of time, during which he actually moved back to his home city. I'd always wanted to leave my own city—I had never felt like I belonged there. Most of my friends already lived in his home city, and my college friends were constantly visiting, so that was where I wanted to be.

We did end up getting married. At the beginning, it was a very good marriage. He was always kind—never a difficult person to be with. We enjoyed our time together immensely. Both our careers were thriving, and we saw the world, skiing in Europe in the winter and spending our summer vacations in London and France.

We had a son together, and we were happy. Or so I thought.

Then, three years into our marriage, he met someone.

✻   ✻   ✻

I had just miscarried my second pregnancy. I was trying to be a good mother to our son, while also wading through my own grief about the miscarriage, when a friend called out of the blue.

"I have some bad news," she said. "I just saw your husband on an airplane with another woman."

So I confronted him. He told me he'd fallen head over heels for another woman.

"Things aren't working out between you and me," he said. "I want to leave."

In the divorce, he took everything. I got nothing. My father had helped him buy a house; he took the house for himself. I moved into our rental house, but before long he wanted my son and me out of the rental house too.

I refused. I said, "You know what? Enough is enough. I'm staying in my house with my son, and I'm not going anywhere."

That's when he started to threaten me. "I'm going to get the police to pick you up," he'd say, "and take you back to your family." It was horrible.

In the meantime, he was paying a ridiculously small amount in child support—about 400 US dollars—in spite of his high salary. I wanted him to at the very least pay for our son's school, so I went to the courts. They did nothing.

Ultimately he left his job. He called my best friend and said, "Tell my ex-wife I'm not going to pay her that much money anymore."

I didn't accept. I went back to court, but once again they couldn't— or wouldn't—help me. He claimed he was out of a job, and it was true. By then he'd lost his second job because he was having an affair with a woman who worked for him. After she got promoted, the company decided that she would stay and he would go.

I was upset. The court cases had dragged on for years with no success. My son was now ten years old, and my dad was taking care of his schooling. I thought the worst of it had passed.

I thought wrong.

I still remember getting the phone call from my lawyer.

He said, "They want your son."

I went crazy. I kept saying, "What do you mean by that? What do you mean?"

"Bring your son down to the courts," he told me. "They just want to interview him."

So I went to the courts, thinking an interview was all they were going to do. But my lawyer wasn't there. He stopped answering my calls and ignored me completely. As I would soon discover, my ex and his legal team had paid my lawyer to make that phone call—and lure me down to the courts.

Once we arrived, they were there to take my son away.

They told my son he was going to have to go to his dad. He was crying, traumatized. I begged them not to do this. How could they take away a little boy who was so attached to his mom? I asked if we could at least go home first.

One of the women who volunteered at the court told me, "Don't do that to your son. He'll be more disturbed if the police come to take him from your house. Let him go with his father, and tell him it's going to be okay. Promise you will see him soon."

I had to sign a paper saying they could take him after four hours.

"It's only on paper," they told me. "You'll see him all the time."

They took him for three and a half months.

During this time, I began volunteering in the courts, helping other women in very tough situations. When you see other people's problems, you start to forget your own. So I worked in the courts every day for a year, never asking for any pay or compensation. After the things I saw, the advice I would give to any young or Generation Z woman is to be smart, and have a prenup. At least then you have a legal document to protect your rights—even though really your fate is in the hands of the individual judge.

I remember one day I saw the judges on my case. They were men, of course. I saw them hug my ex-husband … and I realized they were all friends. My stomach sank. I knew then this was not a normal court, a court that would decide what was in the best interest of a little boy.

> **After the things I saw, the advice I would give to any young or Generation Z woman is to be smart, and have a prenup.**

I was desperate, grasping at straws. I decided to try and move my case to my home city. They kept saying, "But your residency is in another city." I had to keep telling them, "I live there in a rented house. But I'm from here. If I have a house in France, it doesn't mean I'm French."

It took me a year to move the case back to my city. Once I did, I got a woman judge. She told me I would get to see my son every two weeks. No holidays, except in the summer for two weeks. I was allowed to see my son every other Friday.

I was furious. I tried to argue for every week. The judge was horrible and rude, shouting at me in court. You might think a female judge would have more compassion, but sadly that wasn't the case.

So that was how it went. I saw my son every Friday for a few hours. I would pick him up, take him home, have lunch with my parents, then bring him back by nine o'clock. At some point the judge said that when he was with me, he could sleep over. So then I would pick him up on a Friday—and return him Saturday afternoon.

My son is sixteen now. I see him once every two weeks. I lost all my cases—and I wasn't even trying to get him back. All I was asking for were visitation rights, and somehow that became the most difficult and complicated thing.

My son lives with his father and his horrible stepmom. Nobody pays any attention to him. He is constantly on his own. It breaks my heart to see a sixteen-year-old boy crying because he doesn't want to go back to his dad.

We love being with each other. Because we get so little time together, we always end up trying to fix everything in one day. This past summer, when we had two whole weeks together, we bonded a lot. I told him why I didn't trust the courts; how I don't believe it's fair that our fate rests completely in the hands of one judge. When it comes to family court in the Arab world, laws are very open to interpretation. It's all up to one judge and how he happens to feel that day. And your whole life hangs on his decision.

I told my son I'd rather have a better system, or a group of judges who make a decision, not one person.

I told my son I had tried so hard to fight for him.

I told my son none of this was his fault.

I told him that I love him.

Sincerely,
The GCC Fighter

P.S.

No one goes into marriage expecting a bad outcome. Some of us enter into it in love, some after careful calculation. We aren't allowed to officially date, so we do our best with what our culture allows. We talk on the phone, message and meet with chaperones—now it's called a group—but we aren't allowed to live or travel together.

There isn't a logical formula for a perfect marriage; we do our best in hope that it works. But if it doesn't, the legal system must treat us better. In family court, we barely have any female judges—and as the GCC Fighter can attest, the women can sometimes be as bad the men! And as empowering as it is to see women appointed as ministers and members of parliament, it is not enough to simply appoint them. Women must be empowered through legislation.

It's funny how, in construction, we search for new technologies to build faster and better. In education we search for the best methods. We send our children to the best universities for them to learn the latest theories so they can work in this modern international world.

As an Arab woman, I was sent to the United States to study. I returned and worked in a modern workplace. Yet when it comes to my rights as a mother or a wife, these are not at pace with all the modernization around me.

Our religion is beautiful and full of respect. But our whole way of life is changing. Maybe we need to reexamine certain laws protecting women, wives, and mothers.

One other important comment the GCC Fighter made to me was that her father bought all her brothers' houses in France. However, because she is a daughter, he refused to buy her any property. The famous comment Arabic daughters get from fathers and brothers is, "You have a husband. Let him buy you what you need."

The GCC Fighter confessed to me in tears that she feels lucky to be able to take her son with her on summer vacations for two weeks to France. But she has to share a room with her son, while each of her brothers retreats to his private villa.

Our country has made great strides to empower women, and I do see the change and difference under the leadership. I would love to see it more when it comes to divorce and the rights of wives, sisters, and mothers.

Lara, My Daughter

AFTER I RETURNED FROM DOING INTERVIEWS *in a neigh-boring country, my daughter Lara and I sat in my study. We were talking and discussing life, bantering like we usually do. Lara had just returned from working out—she wore her gym clothes, hair up in a ponytail, drinking her healthy green concoction while I sipped my green tea.*

I was talking about how it felt to meet these amazing women, and how I hadn't expected to get quite so emotional.

"I feel so blessed to have done these interviews," I said. "I admire these women. Everyone should admire them! They ought to all be asked to be motivational speakers. We keep seeking only successful businesswomen to represent us and to speak. But these women have passed numerous obstacles. And sadly each of their stories represents us more."

Lara smiled at me from across the study.

"Of course, Mama. Success doesn't mean financial success. I really admire these women you are writing about too. I've enjoyed hearing

about their bravery."

Lara said she believed in the strength of every woman. She told me she had an unfaltering belief that women need to believe in themselves.

I smiled at her.

"Would you write a letter to me, Lara?"

She looked up, surprised. "What am I supposed to write?"

"It's up to you. But everything you just said was lovely. It would make me happy if you wrote it down."

At first she was a bit reluctant. I had to remind her every couple of days. And then one morning, I opened my inbox—and there it was.

⚜ ⚜ ⚜

Dear Mama,

Thank you.

Thank you for what you have done for me, and for instilling this confidence in me. Thank you for showing me I can do whatever I want, no matter my gender.

I see you struggling. I see you working harder than men and not getting rewarded, solely because you are a woman. But I also see the change destined to come. A change that will eradicate the ceaseless inequality and allow equal opportunities; where women are treated with the respect due, not just perceived as bodies or faces, but as having brains and intelligence. We will get the respect and opportunities we deserve.

We have trudged distances and grasped mere glimpses of equality.

> **But I also see the change destined to come. A change that will eradicate the ceaseless inequality and allow equal opportunities.**

But we will not stop here. You have showed me this, Mama, since I was a young girl. Because of that, I will not give up.

So thank you. Thank you for giving women the opportunity to share their stories, women who otherwise would just be shadows. I am proud to call you my mother and to show the world the amazing person you are.

Love,
Lara

P.S.

As I read Lara's letter, tears started rolling down my checks. They were tears of happiness and pride. I thought, Is this what I have instilled in my daughter? *Her beautiful letter shows determination and strength.*

Lara will be going to university in England. She chose to major in science. She wants to do biomedical research, discovering medicines to help people. Sometimes my mother jokingly asks her, "If it's too many years of studying, my dear, when will you have time to get married?" Lara always smiles—and ignores her comment.

It was Lara's words that gave me the idea of talking to Generation Z, as you'll see in the next section. I knew we needed to get their thoughts in the book. After all, they are the future. And what a future! They will not be stopped.

Generation Z

I MET WITH GENERATION Z *and was pleasantly surprised.*

My daughter Lara brought several friends home, and we sat together in the parlor, light pouring in through the skylight overhead. They were such bright, strong, pretty girls, all very trendy, wearing the latest fashions. They came from very different backgrounds. One young woman was covered—she was quiet, but when she talked, she said smart and beautiful things. Another talked about how she no longer wore a hijab after her father experienced a change of heart a few years ago. She spoke more forcefully, with great passion, often interjecting a new thought or idea.

I learned so many things hearing these young women speak. This generation doesn't hold back. They understand they are still in a region with double standards, but they aren't as jaded, and they don't feel a need to follow all the same customs and norms as the generations before them. They have respect for others, but they also hold respect for their own bodies, hearts, and minds.

In other words: they do love themselves. They feel that the sky is the limit, and their gender isn't restricting them like it did my generation. They can see above it—and beyond to what comes next. By recognizing that and working to abolish those standards, they have empowered themselves to fight for the rights they deserve.

Is it social media that is strengthening the women of Generation Z? Could be. We are all now international citizens, observing the world simultaneously through phone apps and lenses. Our culture and walls define us, but these women are defying those walls and reshaping the culture to fit their requirements.

It was a rich and invigorating conversation. I left feeling truly inspired. Though our conversation doesn't follow the epistolary format of the rest of the book, I was so impressed with their insights and bravery that I would be remiss to not include them in Hear Us Speak. *Today's young Arab women are smart, passionate, and empowered. I've shared some of my favorite moments from our conversation below.*

"So tell me about double standards," I said, as we sipped our sodas in the parlor. "Do you feel like you face them?"

"Oh, absolutely," one of the lovely girls replied. "We have to do more to be on the same level as a man—even if the guy puts in half of the effort. Whether that's in parenting or in work, it's a huge double standard if we have to work harder than a man to get the same thing."

"I think if we want to change the double standard," another girl chimed in, "we have to start at home. That's always where real change begins: in the family unit."

They told me how they felt one of first steps to changing society's norms is to adopt a more evolved view on parenting

"If you have kids," they told me, "other people expect you to stay at home with your kids. If you leave them with a childcare provider so that both you and your husband can go to work, then you're seen as a bad parent. But that's our society's restriction."

When I asked about the laws of inheritance—whether in this day and age, they felt women should inherit less than their brothers—they were adamant.

"Absolutely not," one young woman said. "I had this conversation with my dad once, when I had to look at his will. He knows that I have as much potential as my

"I think if we want to change the double standard," another girl chimed in, "we have to start at home. That's always where real change begins: in the family unit."

brothers, or maybe even more, because he sees how hardworking I am. So for my brothers and me, he's given us the same of everything."

Another girl told a different story.

"To be honest," she said, "in my household I've seen a lot of progress. If I think about my life, say, five to eight years ago, it's completely different than it is today. It felt like everything was closed to me but open to my brothers. My father wasn't religious as a child, but when he married my mom and after my oldest brother was born, he went into it really deeply. There was a point where my mom wasn't able to wear anything except black abayas. Everything at home felt very dark.

"But that only went on for a few years. After a while, my dad said, 'I know this is wrong. This is not normal. It's not my life. I wasn't like this, and I don't *want* to be like this.' And, slowly but surely, my family became better educated. I stopped wearing my hijab. My dad recently said to me, 'I did treat you wrong, and I'm sorry for that.'

Now everything is a hundred times better than it was."

"I think everyone needs to be better educated," a third girl added. "Women too. A lot of this stuff gets carried down from mother to daughter. My mother lost her dad at a young age. No one told her 'you should work' or 'you shouldn't.' So she went to work young and had a successful career. But when she got married, my dad said, 'You don't need to work, I'll bring in the money.' And she said, 'Okay.' Because all the women in her family did that: her mother, her grandmother, her sisters, everyone. So she thought it was a normal thing.

"Today my mom says her biggest mistake was that she stopped working. 'Now I have nothing,' she says. 'It's boring.' She always tells me, 'Don't stop studying for anyone. Don't change your life for anyone. And when you get a job, don't stop working. Do what you want to do.'"

"My mom says the same thing," another girl joined in. "She stopped working after she had her second child—my little sister—and now she wishes she'd kept working. Not necessarily for income, but because it's just something to do. I think work gives you something you're passionate about. It's one way to find your purpose in life."

These Generation Z women felt there should be more respect and greater empathy for women. They thought we should not have to continuously fight to get our way—especially when we have to fight other women to achieve our goals.

"One fact that a lot of people neglect," one girl said, "and sometimes avoid entirely is the fact that women are often pitted against women. I think that's a product of our generation, because we're built to be competitive and to hate each other, to bring each other down. We've grown up in this society where not all women are accepted."

"But I don't blame women," another girl interjected. "I think we're all a product of our society, and if a woman tries to keep another woman down, it's because that's what society has done to her in the past. It makes her feel like she needs to fight her way to become the best, because if she isn't the best, she's nothing. If she isn't the top of the chain, then she might as well not be there. Her insecurities are what power her."

They talked about how women should help and support one another, peeling away our insecurities, bit by bit.

"I really appreciate businesswomen like you, Suzy," one girl said, which made me blush. "Because now that we've seen other women conquering things, it gives us hope that we, too, can succeed."

So many times during our conversation, I heard the refrain, "I will not stand down!" This generation of women has ambitions, and nothing can stop them. "Don't change your life for anyone!" they said. Generation Z's rallying cry.

The main theme they all agreed upon was education.

"I feel like education is the number-one weakness in all of this," they said. They felt better and more ubiquitous access to education is what will create the crucial opening that Generation Z women need. It's the gateway to work, which in turn is the gateway to finding their purpose.

One girl said, "Just the other day, our teacher was telling us that the highest percentage of people who take STEM subjects—science and math—are women. But far fewer women go into those professions than men, because before actually doing the job, they're restricted by their families and don't continue on further. So it's mostly women studying it, but when you look at who has actually gotten to the point of being a scientist, engineer, information architect, web developer, or whatever, it's mostly men, because they're allowed to do it more."

We all talked about that for a while, and how we hoped the tide was beginning to turn.

"How about relationships?" I asked. "Do you want to find someone who can take care of you?"

"I think you take care of each other," one of the girls replied. "The most important thing is to invest in your own self-care first. If you can't take care of yourself and love yourself, who can take care of and love you?"

The girls all nodded. One young woman said, "Everyone says relationships are a fifty–fifty thing, but I believe it's a hundred–hundred."

"Agreed," said another. "You have to be able to live by yourself and make sure you are okay being yourself first. Not only okay, but to know who you are and what you want in life—things you won't get through a partner. You have to know you can do it alone. The partner is just there to accompany you on the journey."

"I see," I said, beginning to understand. "It's not about a man taking care of you. You look at it as being partners in life."

"Of course," they said, as if it was the most obvious thing in the world. "It takes two to build a bridge."

For Generation Z, marriage was not about the expectation that a husband care for his wife financially and emotionally. They wanted to find a partner where they both understood and respected one another.

"What if you fall in love," I said, playing devil's advocate, "and then the guy says, 'I love you, I love you, I love you. Look how beautiful you are! You're so beautiful, I want you to cover yourself. Only I get to see your beauty.'"

One of the young women smiled.

"My granddad always tells me, 'If you had a beautiful flower, why would you cover it?'"

I told her I thought that was very sweet.

"I would never let a man tell me to cover myself," said another one of the girls. "If I'm going to do anything for my religion, it's going to be for me and my religion. And that's between me and God. People have a way of trying to twist religion to make it very extreme."

"But do you all love Islam?" I said.

They agreed unanimously.

"But what Islam means to each person is different," said one girl. "People shouldn't inflict what they believe on other people."

"We see a beautiful side of Islam in this country," said another. "Which it is. Islam is a very beautiful religion. And the Islam that we all know? It gives people a fair chance. You cannot beat a woman up in the Islam that we know. You cannot physically abuse her in the Islam that we know.

"But in the Islam that people twist for their benefit? Anything is possible."

I asked them what would they do if their husband came home one day and said, "Listen, I love you, but I need to marry another woman and have a second wife."

"I'm out," said one girl, and we all laughed.

"None of you would accept that?" I asked.

They shook their heads.

"What I would say to my husband is, 'Go, the door is open.'"

We talked about people who point to the Quran and say men can have more than one wife, as long as they treat each of them equally. They felt this was a misinterpretation of Islam.

"How can you love something and then love something else exactly equal amounts? You cannot treat people equally with love. You cannot love them in the same way. Even in the Quran it says, 'I tell you it is impossible.'"

"What if you ended up marrying a foreign man?" I asked. "Would your parents accept it?"

"I don't feel like my parents would say no straight away," one girl answered. "But they'd have to see that he was the right person. They'd ask, 'Does he treat you properly? Is he generous with you? Would he be able to support you through everything?'"

The words of these beautiful, strong, and confident young women filled me with pride! I have no doubt they will be achievers who do things most women in our generation haven't been able to do. We were conditioned to believe we have to comply with norms. Although a few of us defied and conquered, in general we complied— while deep down we remained resentful, without fully understanding why.

I asked them, "Do you still think we are living in a patriarchal society?"

"Yes."

"But you do see it's changing?"

"Slowly. I think our generation is going to create the change."

"Last but not least," I said, "if you have a family someday, and you had both daughters and sons, would you try to tell your husband to treat all your children equal?"

"Not try," said one young woman. "I *will*."

And I knew then that the future of the Arab world is in good hands.

Epilogue: A Brighter Tomorrow

WHEN I STARTED WRITING THIS BOOK, I assumed I would be writing about abused women. As I began planning the interviews, I braced myself for stories that were depressing and horrifying. I was imagining the worst.

Then the actual work began. I travelled to other countries and around on my own, meeting and speaking to women. I received emails, phone calls, and letters putting me in touch with women I had never met. "She has the most amazing story," people would tell me. "You must speak to her." Women I'd known or worked with came to my office and said, "Suzy, let me tell you what I survived. You won't even believe it."

I won't lie. In many cases, the horror was true. But what I was surprised to discover was the strength of these magnificent women.

Here were individuals who should be admired, heard, and discussed. They persevered against all odds and chose love over hate. These women stood up and fought for their rights rather than remain submissive and give up to misery and anger.

I was overwhelmed by the resilience of these women. They were soldiers fighting for their country, only they had never received any recognition or medals of honor. And yet, for themselves and their children, they were winning battles every day.

Hear Us Speak is for those women—the ones we know about and the ones we don't. I hope this book is a small gesture to show the world what women are capable of, and how mothers only want to see their offspring shine with happiness and purpose.

I bow my head to these women, and *all* women. As my daughter Lara says, "Change is coming."

Hear us speak, feel our love and pain—and carry our hope for a brighter tomorrow.

Suzy Kanoo